# BIG
## NEEDLES
## CHUNKY
## KNITS

# BIG
## NEEDLES
## CHUNKY
## KNITS

**Helgrid van Impelen**

*Photography: Katja Schubert*

# Contents

**Big needles** | Fast results — 6
**Tools and equipment** | Handy checklist — 8
**Before you begin** | Tips for success — 10

## City knits

**Cosmopolitan colour** | Ribbed jumper with matching mittens — 14
**Uptown style** | Open coat with tie belt — 18
**Casual duo** | Smooth colour-block jumper with long scarf — 22
**City slicker** | Poncho with wristwarmers — 28
**All wrapped up** | Casual wrap — 32
**Urban chic** | Cosy top with matching cowl — 36
**Streetwise cool** | Long block-stripe cardigan — 40

## Country style

**Rustic charm** | Hooded jacket with toggles — 48
**Spring break** | Long top with cowl, wristwarmers and hat — 56
**Shades of autumn** | Long coat with cable pattern — 62
**Winter warmers** | Poncho with hat and legwarmers — 68
**Subtle neutrals** | Jumper with hat and child's shoulder warmer — 72
**Woodland walk** | Casual ribbed jacket — 78
**Nature lover** | Mini-waistcoat in moss stitch — 82
**Riverside ramble** | Simple body warmer — 86

## Home comforts

**Lazy days** | Stocking-stitch jumper with scarf — 90
**Sheer elegance** | Pretty wrapover cardigan — 94
**Soft and silky** | Open jacket with moss-stitch borders and matching scarf — 98
**Relax to the max** | Long hooded coat — 102
**Snuggle up** | Two-tone jumper with broad stripes — 106
**Light as air** | Fluffy jumper with giant cable — 110
**Easy earth tones** | Long coat with multi-coloured stripes and child's jumper — 114
**Luxurious lace** | Poncho with matching legwarmers — 122

## Basic techniques

Casting on — 128
Casting off — 129
Slipping stitches off the needle — 129
Slipping stitches — 130
Reading charts — 131
Measuring tension — 131
Altering patterns — 132
Increasing — 132
Decreasing — 134
Cables — 135
Horizontal inset pocket — 136
Pom-poms — 137
Working on a set of five double-pointed needles — 138
Finishing — 138
Cast-off horizontal buttonhole — 139
Joining seams — 140
Steaming and pressing — 141

# Big Needles

*FAST RESULTS*

The joy of knitting begins before you cast on a single stitch. Can you imagine a more inviting sight than a basket filled to overflowing with balls of thick mohair, luxurious alpaca, sleek silk, or flawless, matt cotton, in shades ranging from subtle natural hues to vivid, eye-popping colours? And stuck in the middle of this fleecy jumble, there is a pair of smooth, chunky bamboo needles, just waiting for you to pick them up and put them to use.

Then, when you take up those needles and start to work, you know you can put aside the worries of the day and lose yourself in an activity that is both practical and creative. The pleasure of knitting is seasoned by the anticipation of seeing – and feeling – the finished article.

And best of all is that sense of achievement you have when friends admire a finished creation, and you can say, "I knitted it myself!"

This book will help you to achieve all this quickly and easily, because – depending on the project – the chunky yarns and big needles mean that you can achieve real success in just a few hours.

In the first section, "City knits", the focus is on sophisticated designs with subtle colour accents – perfect choices for shopping, visiting a gallery or meeting friends for lunch. "Country style" has a rustic flavour, with natural shades of beige, chocolate and aubergine. You'll find capes, ponchos and cardigans to keep out the chill in style. "Home comforts" is a delicious collection of delicate pastel shades, silky, sensuous yarns, and relaxed styles, tailor-made for cosy evenings curled up on the sofa.

Whether you are a beginner, a returner, or an expert, there's something for you here. Each project's difficulty level is graded from 1 to 4 – just look out for the balls of yarn in the materials box at the start of each project. And as well as easy-to-follow patterns and inspirational photos, you'll also find plenty of tips and useful information on tools, techniques, and yarns.

I wish you inspiration, relaxation – and fun!

*Helgrid van Impelen*

Helgrid van Impelen

# Tools and equipment

*HANDY CHECKLIST*

 **Sharp- and blunt-ended sewing needles** | Tapestry and yarn needles are useful for sewing up projects, because their blunt ends won't damage delicate wool fibres. Use a sharp-ended needle to secure darned-in ends or to attach trimmings. Make sure you choose a needle with an eye that is large enough for the yarn you're using, so that you don't split or damage the yarn.

 **Cable needle** | Cable needles have a point at each end and a small, V-shaped bend, or kink, in the middle. The kink prevents stitches from sliding away when knitting cable patterns. Cable needles are available in various sizes; select needles that are closest in size to the needles you are using for the rest of your knitting.

 **Stitch holder** | You should always try to keep enough stitch holders handy – they are especially useful when you need to set aside stitches at shoulders, necklines, or pockets to work on later. If you run out of stitch holders, you can use spare double-pointed needles, but be careful, as stitches can easily slide off needles without stitch stoppers.

**Row counter** | A row counter helps you to keep track of how many rows you have completed as you knit. You can slip it on to one of your needles or attach it to your work with a safety pin. Some counters have to be manually changed every time you finish a row; others are just "clicked" at the end of each row. Either way, they only work if you remember to use them!

 **Tape measure** | Before you start a project, use a tape measure to take the body measurements of the person you are knitting for, or to compare the measurements of the project with an existing article of clothing that you know fits well. During the project, keep a tape measure handy to check tension or to measure your knitting.

**Stitch markers** | Use a stitch marker to mark the beginning and end of a panel of stitches, or to identity the end of each row when you are working in the round. If you don't have any stitch markers to hand, you could use small safety pins or a short length of contrasting coloured yarn.

**Scissors** | You should always keep a small pair of good-quality needlecraft scissors handy, for cutting off yarn and trimming ends. Sharp, short-bladed scissors are best: they allow you to snip really close to the work, keeping darned-in ends neater when you finish a seam.

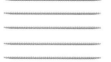

**Double-pointed needles** | Designed so that stitches can be slipped on and off at both ends, double-pointed needles (also called dpns) are used for circular knitting, or for tubes. They are short needles that can only accommodate a small number of stitches, making them the best option for knitting very narrow tubes, such as gloves or socks. Many knitters find that wooden and bamboo double-pointed needles are easier to work with as they are less slippery than metal or plastic needles.

**Circular needles** | Circular needles consist of a flexible cord that attaches to needles at either end. They are mainly used for knitting tubular items, such as hats, socks, or seamless sleeves. You can work a piece of flat knitting with circular needles; just turn your needles around after every row instead of working in the round. Long circular needles are also used for knitting wide or heavy items, such as blankets, because the weight of the work is taken by the cord and it can sit in your lap, rather than hanging off the ends of standard needles, putting strain on your wrists. This makes it more comfortable to knit as your work gets heavier. Interchangeable circular needles are worth investing in if you find you prefer to use circular needles for all your projects. Circular needle sets are made up of connecting tubes of various lengths, and a selection of different-sized needles.

# Before you begin

*TIPS FOR SUCCESS*

**Before you begin** | While it is true that thick yarns are easier to knit and that even beginners can achieve success in a short space of time, you will enjoy the projects more and achieve even better results if you keep in mind a few basic guidelines.

**Plan for success** | If you are new to working with thick yarns, think about which styles suit your figure and choose an appropriate pattern. Thick yarns can give a bulkier result than thinner ones. So, for larger sizes, opt for casual, one-size styles and avoid designs with tight sleeves or small armholes. For a flattering outline, go for patterns with few seams. If you are not sure which size to choose, compare the pattern measurements with those of a similar garment from your wardrobe that you know fits well.

**Yarn quantities** | The chunkier the yarn and the larger the needles, the more yarn you will need. Buying a less expensive yarn does not always turn out to be the bargain it seemed to be. A higher-quality, more expensive yarn often keeps its looks longer and is more hard-wearing than a cheaper option. Choose a classic style and colourway and enjoy wearing your garment for years to come.

**Chunky yarns are heavy** | Keep in mind that chunky yarns can be quite heavy once they are knitted up. A knitted coat or long jacket will always stretch a little because of the sheer weight of the yarn. This has been taken into account when calculating the lengths of the designs in this book.

**Alta Moda for best results** | The Alta Moda yarns from Lana Grossa used for some of the designs in this book are particularly good for very big stitches. The yarn structure looks like a thinner version of a tube from a French knitter. This gives maximum volume from a comparatively small quantity of yarn. Knitwear made from Alta Moda feels lighter and airier than those made from spun yarns but is just as warm and cosy.

**Stay loose** | Choose larger rather than smaller needle sizes and remember to keep your knitting loose. Particularly fleecy yarns should be knitted with very big stitches. If the stitches are too close together, the surface can look slightly matted, the yarn will not look its best, and the finished garment will be stiff.

**Avoid seams** | Knit as far as possible in a single piece, so that you avoid seams in your garment. Thick seams can be ugly and uncomfortable, they add bulk, and can give a lumpy outline. Always knit sleeves on a set of circular or double-pointed needles. Make jackets without side seams and knit shoulder seams together, rather than sewing them.

**Less is more** | Working with thick yarns and big needles will give your knits a strong visual appeal. There is often no need for fancy stitches – all you need to create a striking, on-trend garment are a few basic knitting techniques and a strong sense of colour. If you do choose to use a fancy stitch, don't make it too detailed or fussy, or it will lessen the visual impact of your item.

# City knits

AS YOU SOAK UP THE LAST OF THE AUTUMN SUN AT YOUR FAVOURITE PAVEMENT CAFÉ, ALL YOU NEED TO KEEP OUT THE CHILL IS A FROTHY CAPPUCINO AND A WARM, FLEECY KNIT!

# Cosmopolitan colour

*RIBBED JUMPER WITH MATCHING MITTENS*

## FOR THE JUMPER

### TENSION
7 stitches and 26 rows in fisherman's rib on 12mm (UKn/a/US17) needles = 10cm (4in) square.

### STITCHES
**Fisherman's rib** | In all rows slip the purl stitches purlwise, yarn over needle, and knit the plain stitches together with the yarn over from the previous row. Knit as loosely as possible.
**Edge stitch** | Work the first and last stitches of every row knitwise.

**Back and front** | The back and front are identical. Cast on 35 stitches and work the first row as a wrong-side row as follows:
Knit 1 purl 1 alternately, ending with a knit stitch.
Continue in fisherman's rib:
Row 1 (right-side row): Knit 1 (edge stitch), *knit 1, yarn over, slip 1 purlwise*; repeat from * to *, ending with knit 1 and 1 edge stitch.
Row 2 (wrong-side row): Knit 1, * yarn over, slip 1 purlwise, knit 1 together with the yarn over in the previous row*; repeat from * to *, ending with yarn over, slip 1 purlwise, and 1 edge stitch.
Row 3: Knit 1, *knit 1 together with the yarn over in the previous row, yarn over, slip 1 purlwise *; repeat from * to * ending with knit 1 together with yarn over in the previous row and 1 edge stitch.

**RIBBED JUMPER WITH MATCHING MITTENS**
**One size**
**Style:** loose, but not oversized

### MATERIALS
- 650g Lana Grossa Alta Moda Super Baby (60m/50g; 67% wool, 30% alpaca, 3% polyamide) in orange red (col. 18) for jumper and leftover yarn for mittens (single yarn)
- 100g Lana Grossa Merino Air (130m/50g; 90% wool, 10% polyamide) in anthracite (col. 03), for mittens (yarn will be worked double)
- 12mm (UKn/a/US17) circular needles, 60 and 80cm (24 and 32in) long, for jumper
- Set of 7mm (UK2/US10½) double-pointed needles for mittens
- Stitch holder or spare needle

Repeat rows 2 and 3 until work measures
55cm (21½in).

**Shoulders** | When work measures 55cm (21½in),
cast off the outer 10 stitches at both edges and
knit the stand-up collar on the central 15 stitches.

**Collar** | Work 6cm (2⅜in) in fisherman's rib and
cast off all stitches loosely.

**Join the shoulder and collar seams** | Place the
front and back right sides together and on each
side sew the shoulder and collar together in a
single, continuous seam.

**Armholes** | Measure 21cm (8¼in) down from
the shoulder seams and mark the position of the
armholes.

**Sleeves** | Cast on 17 stitches and start with a
wrong-side row: work 1 row in knit 1 purl 1 rib,
starting with knit 1.
Then work in fisherman's rib pattern, as
described for the back and front.

**Sleeve increases** | Increase 1 stitch at each end
of every 6th right-side row 6 times (29 stitches).
Increase by working make 1 between the first
two stitches and the last two stitches of the row
by picking up the horizontal strand between the
stitches and knitting into the back of it. When
work measures 50cm (19½in), cast off all stitches
loosely. The sleeve length is generous, so that
the cuffs can be turned up.

**Finishing** | Sew the top edge of the sleeve to the
back and front between the markers. Then,
starting from the bottom edge, join the front and
back together and the sleeve seam from the
armhole down to the bottom edge in one

continuous seam. Repeat on the other side of the
garment. Darn in all the ends.

**FOR THE MITTENS**
TENSION
12 stitches and 16 rows in stocking stitch with
double yarn on 7mm (UK2/US10½) needles
= 10cm (4in) square.

STITCHES
**Stocking stitch in rounds** | Knit all stitches.
**Rib border** | Knit 1 purl 1 alternately.

**Border** | With two strands of anthracite yarn
together and the set of double-pointed needles,
cast on 20 stitches and distribute evenly between
the needles.
Work 9cm (3½in) in rounds in single rib.
Work 3 rounds in stocking stitch, then start
increasing for the thumb.

**Thumb** | 1st increase: Increase 1 stitch at each
side by knitting into the strand between the first
two stitches and the last two stitches of the
round. Knit these stitches through the back of the
loop in the next round to prevent holes from
appearing in the work.
Work 2 rounds in stocking stitch.
2nd increase: Increase 1 stitch at each side by
knitting into the strand between the second and
third stitches and between the second and third
stitches from the end of the round. Knit these
stitches through the back of the loop in the next
round to prevent holes from appearing in the work.
Work 2 rounds in stocking stitch.
3rd increase: Increase 1 stitch at each side by
knitting into the strand between the third and
fourth stitches and between the third and fourth
stitches from the end of the round (26 stitches).
Knit these stitches through the back of the loop

in the next round to prevent holes from appearing in the work.
Work 2 rounds in stocking stitch.

**Thumb** | Slip the first 3 stitches of the first needle and the last three stitches of the last needle onto safety pins.

**Hand** | Join the remaining 20 stitches into a round, distributing the stitches evenly. Work 8cm (3¼in) stocking stitch in rounds, then change colour to orange red.

**Top** | Decrease for the top as follows:
*Knit 1, slip 1, knit 1, pass slipped stitch over (see page 134), knit 4, knit 2 together, knit 1*. Repeat from * to *.
Knit one round on these 16 stitches.
Next row: *Knit 1, slip 1, knit 1, pass slipped stitch over, knit 2, knit 2 together, knit 1*. Repeat from * to *.
Knit one round on these 12 stitches.
Next row: *Knit 1, slip 1, knit 1, pass slipped stitch over, knit 2 together, knit 1*. Repeat from * to *.
(8 stitches remain).
Cut off the yarn, thread the end through all the stitches, pull tight and darn in on the inside.

**Thumb** | Arrange the 6 stitches from the safety pins with 2 stitches on each of three needles, join into a round and pick up and knit 1 stitch between the last and first stitches of the round, next to the hand.
On these 7 stitches work 8cm (3¼in) stocking stitch in rounds. On the last round knit 2 together 3 times, knit 1 (4 stitches remain).
Cut off the yarn, thread the end through all the stitches, pull tight and darn in on the inside.

**Finishing** | Draw the stitches together firmly where the hand joins the thumb. Darn in all the ends.
Make the second mitten in the same way.

# Pattern

*RIBBED JUMPER*

**PATTERN DIAGRAM**
Measurements in cm (in)

# Uptown style

*OPEN COAT WITH TIE BELT*

**TENSION**
5.5 stitches and 20 rows in fisherman's rib on 12mm (UKn/a/US17) needles = 10cm (4in) square.

**STITCHES**
**Fisherman's rib** | Row 1 (right-side row): Knit 1 (edge stitch), *knit 1, yarn over, slip 1 purlwise*; repeat from * to *, ending with knit 1, knit 1 (edge stitch).
Row 2 (wrong-side row): Knit 1 (edge stitch), * yarn over, slip 1 purlwise, knit 1 stitch together with the yarn over from the previous row*; repeat from * to *, ending with yarn over, slip 1 purlwise, knit 1 (edge stitch).
Row 3: Knit 1, *knit 1 together with the yarn over in the previous row, yarn over , slip 1 purlwise *; repeat from * to * ending with knit 1 together with yarn over in the previous row and 1 edge stitch.
Repeat rows 2 and 3.
Knit as loosely as possible.

**Edge stitches** | Work the first and last stitches of every row knitwise.

**OPEN COAT WITH TIE BELT**
Size: S–M
**Style:** narrow, figure-hugging.
A striking pattern that looks especially good on taller figures. Newly knitted, the length is 100cm (40in), but because of the stitch used and the weight of the yarn, it will stretch to as much as 115cm (46in).

**MATERIALS**
- 1100g Classic Elite Toboggan (80m/100g; 70% merino, 30% alpaca) in ebony (col. 6713)
- 12mm (UKn/a/US17) circular needle 100cm (40in) long
- Set of 10mm (UK000/US15) double-pointed needles
- 8mm (UK0/USL-11) crochet hook
- Stitch markers or safety pins
- Stitch holders or spare needles

# Pattern

**PATTERN DIAGRAM**
Measurements in cm (in).

## TO MAKE

**Back and front** | The coat is knitted in one piece in long rows up to the armholes. On a 12mm circular needle cast on 65 stitches.
Knit the 1st row (wrong-side row) as follows: Knit 1 (edge stitch), then purl 1, knit 1 alternately, ending with knit 1 (edge stitch).
Continue in fisherman's rib until work measures 78cm (31½in). Then divide the 65 stitches into the fronts and back as follows:

18 stitches for the right front, 29 stitches for the back and 18 stitches for the left front. Mark the imaginary seams with stitch markers or safety pins.

**Back armholes** | Finish the back first. Cast off the first 2 stitches of the next two rows. Work a further 22cm (8⅝in) in fisherman's rib on the remaining 25 stitches.

**Shoulders and back neck** | When work measures 100cm (40in), work 8 stitches, cast off the centre 9 stitches and work to the end of the row.
In the following row, cast off the remaining 8 stitches for the shoulder, then cast off the 8 stitches at the other side.

**Front armhole and shoulder** | Finish the fronts separately.
At the start of the row (armhole edge), cast off 1 stitch and continue working on the remaining 17 stitches.
When work measures 100cm (40in), cast off the first 4 stitches at the neck edge (13 stitches remain).
At the armhole edge, cast off 8 stitches for the shoulder and slip the remaining 5 stitches onto a holder for the collar.

**Join the shoulder seams** | Turn the coat to the wrong side and sew the shoulders together or graft together on the right side.

**Collar** | Starting with the left front, with wrong side facing, knit the 5 stitches from the holder, pick up 9 stitches along the back neck and knit the 5 stitches from the holder of the right front (19 stitches).
Continue in fisherman's rib, so that the stitches from the holders continue the pattern correctly.
When the collar measures 12cm (4¾in), cast off all stitches loosely.

**Sleeves** | Cast on 15 stitches and work a wrong-side row in knit 1 purl 1 rib. Continue in fisherman's rib. Work the first and last stitches of each row as a knit 1 edge stitch.

Increase 1 stitch at each end of every 12th row 6 times (27 stitches).
When work measures 50cm (19½in), cast off all stitches loosely.

**Belt** | For the belt, work on 2 needles from the set of 10mm double-pointed needles. Cast on 5 stitches and work in knit 1 purl 1 rib. Continue in rib until the work measures 170cm (67in), then cast off all stitches.

**Belt loops** | With an 8mm crochet hook, on the side seam about 13cm (5¼in) below the armhole, insert the hook into a knit stitch, crochet 8 chain and fasten off with a slip stitch into a knit stitch 8cm (3¼in) below the start of the loop.
Thread the ends through to the inside and darn them in.
Make a second loop on the other side seam.

**Making up** | Sew in the sleeves. Darn in all the ends.

Instead of the knitted belt, you could wear a narrow leather belt with your long coat instead. Very chic and sleek!

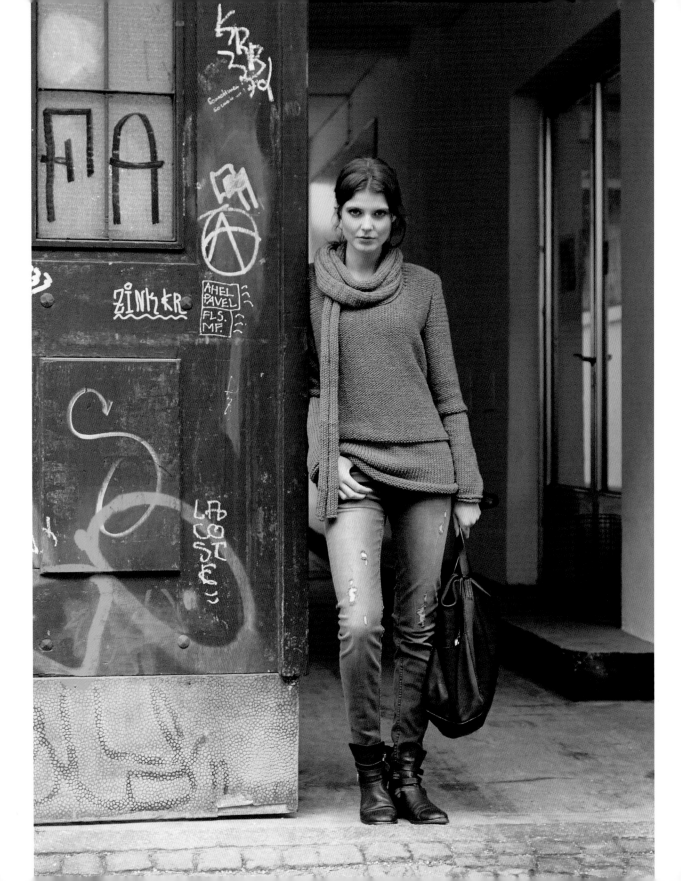

# Casual duo

*SMOOTH COLOUR-BLOCK JUMPER
WITH LONG SCARF*

## TENSION

13 stitches and 19 rows in stocking stitch on 7mm (UK2/US10½) needles = 10cm (4in) square.

## STITCHES

**Stocking stitch** | In rows: On right-side rows knit all stitches, on wrong-side rows purl all stitches. In rounds: Knit all stitches.

**Reverse stocking stitch** | In rows: On right-side rows purl all stitches, on wrong-side rows knit all stitches.
In rounds: Purl all stitches.

## FOR THE JUMPER

**Back and front** | The jumper is knitted in one piece in rounds up to the armholes. With 7mm circular needle and light red yarn, cast on 120 (128:136) stitches and join into a round.

For the rolled edge, work 3 rounds stocking stitch and one round purl, then continue in stocking stitch.

Mark the imaginary side seams with stitch markers or safety pins. The front and back each consist of 60 (64:68) stitches. The rounds begin at the right edge of the front.

When work measures 15cm (6in), change to dark grey and reverse stocking stitch, so that the purl stitches can now be seen on the outside (or right side) of the work.

**SMOOTH COLOUR-BLOCK JUMPER WITH LONG SCARF**
**Sizes S, M, L**
Measurements for size S are in front of brackets: sizes M and L are inside brackets (M:L). If only one measurement is given, it applies to all sizes.
**Style:** close-fitting
**Scarf:** 240cm (94½in) long and 17cm (6¾in) wide

## MATERIALS

- 450 (500:550)g Lana Grossa Super Bingo (55m/50g; 100% wool) in dark grey marl (col. 25) and 200 (200:250)g in light red (col. 46) for jumper; 100g each in dark grey and light red for scarf
- 7mm (UK2/US10½) circular needles 60 and 80cm (24 and 32in) long
- Set of 7mm (UK2/US10½) double-pointed needles
- Stitch holders or spare needles
- Stitch markers or safety pins

# Pattern

**PATTERN DIAGRAM**
Measurements in cm (in).

4.5 (1¾)

8 (9:11)
(3½ (3⅝:4⅜))

22 (8⅝)

8 (9:11)
(3½ (3½:4⅜))

4.5 (1¾)

2 (¾)

14 (5½)

20 (21:22)
(7⅞ (8¼:8⅝))

Front and back

68 (26¾)

52 (20½)

48 (47:46)
(18½ (18½:18⅛))

47 (49:53)
(18⅛ (19½:20½))

32 (34:36)
(12½ (13⅜:14¼))

15 (16:17)
(6 (6¼:6⅝))

Sleeve

44 (17⅞)

55 (60:61)
(23⅜ (23⅝:24))

22 (24:26)
(8⅝ (9½:10¼))

**Decrease for waistline** | The jumper is slightly waisted. For this, stitches are decreased at both sides.

When the work measures 21cm (8¼in), purl together the second and third stitches and the third-last and second-last stitches of the front and back, i.e. decrease a total of 4 stitches in this round.

Repeat these decreases twice more in every following 4th round (108 (116:124) stitches remain).

Work 4 rounds in reverse stocking stitch then increase to replace the previous decreases by purling into the front and back of the second and second-last stitches of the front and back. Repeat the increases twice more in every following 4th round, until there are once again 120 (128:136) stitches on the needle.

**Divide for back and front** | When work measures 48 (47:46)cm (18⅞ (18½:18⅛)in), divide for the armholes. The back and front are finished separately and worked in rows.

Divide the stitches into 60 (64:68) stitches each for the front and back. Work the back first.

**Armholes** | Cast off 3 stitches at the start of the next 2 rows. Then decrease at each side 2 stitches once and 1 stitch once (48 (52:56) stitches remain on the needle).

Continue without further shaping until back measures 66cm (26in).

**Back neck** | When back measures 66cm (26in), slip the centre 18 stitches onto a spare needle or stitch holder.

Finish the right and left sides of the back separately by casting off at the neck edge on every other row 3 stitches once and 2 stitches once. When back measures 68cm (26¾in), slip the remaining 10 (12:14) stitches onto holders for the shoulders. They will later be knitted together with the shoulder stitches of the front.

**Front neck** | When front measures 52cm (20½in), slip the centre 16 stitches onto a spare needle or a stitch holder. Finish the right and left sides of the front separately by casting off at the neck edge on every other row 2 stitches twice and 1 stitch twice.

When fronts measure 68cm (26¾in), slip the remaining shoulder stitches onto stitch holders, as for the back.

**Join the shoulder seams** | Turn the jumper to the wrong side and join one shoulder seam by knitting together 1 stitch of the back and 1 stitch of the front shoulder. Next row: cast off all stitches. Join the second shoulder seam in the same way.

Alternatively, the shoulder stitches can be grafted together or cast off and sewn up later.

**Neck border** | On the set of double-pointed needles, with the right side of the work facing you and starting at the back right shoulder, pick up 5 stitches from the cast-off edge, 18 stitches from the back neck stitch holder, 5 stitches from the cast-off edge at the other side, 14 stitches down the left side of the front neck opening, 6 cast-off stitches, 16 stitches from the holder, 6 cast-off stitches and 14 stitches up the right side of the front neck opening (84 stitches). Work 2 rows stocking stitch, then cast off all stitches loosely.

**Sleeves** | The sleeves are knitted in rounds on the set of 7mm double-pointed needles. Cast on 28 (31:34) stitches in light red, divide evenly between the needles and work the rolled edge as described for the jumper. Mark the imaginary seam.

After the rolled edge, increase on every 10th round by knitting into the strand between the second and third stitches and between the third-last and second-last stitches. Repeat 6 more times, until there are 42 (45:48) stitches on the needles.

When the work measures 25cm (10in), change to dark grey and reverse stocking stitch.

**Sleeve top** | When work measures 44cm (17³⁄₈in) change to working in rows. Because of the curve of the top, it is best to begin by continuing to work on two or three of the double-pointed needles. Later, when there are fewer stitches on the needle, one needle will be enough.

Cast off 3 stitches at the beginning of the next two rows (36 (39:42) stitches remain).

Then at each side, cast off 2 stitches once and 1 stitch three times (26 (29:32) stitches remain). Work 9 (10:11)cm (3⁵⁄₈ (4:4³⁄₈)in) without shaping, then cast off at each end of the next 6 rows:

Size S: cast off 1–0–1–2–3–3 stitches. On the next row cast off the remaining 6 stitches.

Size M: cast off 1–1–1–2–3–3 and the remaining 7 stitches on the next row.

Size L: cast off 1–1–1–2–3–4 and the remaining 8 stitches on the next row.

**Finishing** | Sew in the sleeves. Darn in all the ends. Lightly steam the jumper or leave to dry under a damp cloth.

**FOR THE LONG SCARF**

With 7mm circular needle and dark grey, cast on 22 stitches and work in stocking stitch in rows. Work the first stitch of every row as an edge stitch: on right-side rows slip the stitch knitwise, on wrong-side rows purlwise.

Change colour after every 14 rows, knitting broad stripes in light red and dark grey.

When work measures 120cm (47in) after a light red stripe, reduce the width of the stripes and work 2 rows in dark grey and 2 rows in light red alternately. Do not cut off the yarn at the end of the narrow stripes, work it in at the edge.

When work measures 240cm (94½in) after a light red stripe, knit a small rolled edge in dark grey, as described for the jumper on page 23, and cast off all stitches.

Darn in the ends and steam the scarf lightly. It will roll up a little; this effect is deliberate.

# City slicker

*PONCHO WITH WRISTWARMERS*

## TENSION
14 stitches and 20 rows in stocking stitch on 6mm (UK4/US10) needles = 10cm (4in) square.

## STITCHES
**Stocking stitch** | In rounds knit all stitches.
**Ribbed border** | Knit 1 purl 1 alternately.
**Zigzag pattern** | Work the zigzag pattern from the chart over 16 stitches. The figures to the right of the chart refer to the pattern rounds. On the even-numbered rounds in between, knit all stitches. Keep repeating rounds 1–28.

## FOR THE PONCHO
The poncho is knitted in one piece in rounds from the top down. It starts at the roll collar with a ribbed border and finishes at the hem, also with a small ribbed border. The rounds start between the left arm and the back. Mark the beginning of the round with a stitch marker or safety pin. When you reach the appropriate number of stitches, change to the next-longest needle.

**Roll collar** | With the set of double-pointed needles, cast on 76 stitches and work 15cm (6in) in knit 1 purl 1 rib. In the next round, change to stocking stitch and increase 14 stitches, evenly distributed (90 stitches).

**Divide the stitches** | Divide the stitches into four areas: 29 stitches for the back, 16 stitches for the right arm, 29 stitches for the front and 16 stitches for the left arm.
To make it easier to keep track, mark the four areas with stitch markers.
Work the zigzag pattern according to the chart on page 31, over the centre 16 stitches of the front.

### PONCHO WITH WRISTWARMERS
One size
**Style:** generous but not full

### MATERIALS
- 600g Trendsetter Yarns Merino 12 (124m/100g; 100% merino wool) in light pearl for the poncho and 124m for the wrist-warmers
- 6mm (UK4/US10) circular needles, 60 and 80cm (24 and 32in) long
- Set of 6mm (UK4/US10) double-pointed needles
- Stitch markers or safety pins
- Stitch holders or cable needles

**Increases** | After two rounds, begin increasing. Work the increases with a yarn over before and after each of the 16 sleeve stitches. Increase 4 stitches per round, 5 times in successive rounds (90 + 20 = 110 stitches) and 8 times in every other round (110 + 32 = 142 stitches). Then increase 5 times in every 5th round, so that when you reach the arm openings, there are 162 stitches in total on the needle.

**Arm openings** | When work measures 45cm (17¾in), start the arm openings. At this point you will have 65 stitches for the back, 16 stitches for the right arm, 65 stitches for the front and 16 stitches for the left arm.
The arm openings will be positioned on either side of the centre 51 stitches of the front, with 7 stitches to the right and left of them. Work one more round without any increases, ending this round at 7 stitches before the end of the front section, ready to start the arm openings.
Work in rows, starting at the left arm opening with a right-side row: Knit 7 stitches to the right of the opening, 16 stitches of the left sleeve, 65 stitches across the back, 16 stitches of the right sleeve and 7 stitches to the left of the other opening.
Turn and work the wrong-side row.
Slip the centre front 51 stitches onto a holder. Work 25cm (10in), remembering to increase either side of the sleeves as before, and continue increasing in every 5th row (another 10 × 4 stitches = 40 stitches; total stitch count = 202).
Slip the stitches onto a spare needle and work 25cm (10in) on the 51 stitches between the openings, including the zigzag pattern.
Now return all the stitches to the circular needle and work in rounds. Continue without further increasing until the work measures 70cm (27½in).

**Bottom border** | Work 10cm (4in) in rib, then cast off all stitches loosely.

**Arm opening borders** | With the circular needle, pick up 45 stitches along one edge of the opening and work 2cm (¾in) in rib, starting and ending with a knit stitch. Cast off all stitches. Work the other 3 borders in the same way.
Sew the narrow edges of the borders to the fronts, with the top layer pointing towards the side and the lower layer towards the centre of the garment.

**Finishing** | Darn in all the ends.

## FOR THE WRIST-WARMERS

On the set of 6mm double-pointed needles, cast on 28 stitches and distribute evenly between the needles. Work 5cm (2in) in knit 1 purl 1 rib.
For the thumb opening, change to working in rows. Knit into the front and back of the last stitch of the last needle, so that the rows begin and end with a knit stitch.
Work 6cm (2⅜in) (total length 11cm (4⅜in)), then cast off the extra stitch and change back to working in rounds.
When work measures 22cm (8¾in) and again at 28cm (11¼in), increase by working make 1 in the strands before and after the 6th stitch for the right wrist-warmer and before and after the 22nd stitch for the left wrist-warmer (32 stitches).
When work measures 34cm (13⅝in), cast off all stitches loosely and sew in the ends.

# Chart and pattern

*PONCHO WITH WRISTWARMERS*

## CHART
Zigzag pattern

## Key:

 = Knit 1

 = Twist 2 right: slip 1 stitch onto a cable needle and hold at back of work, slip the next stitch purlwise with the yarn behind the stitch, then knit the stitch from the cable needle.

= Twist 2 left: slip 1 stitch onto a cable needle and hold at front of work, knit the next stitch, then slip the stitch from the cable needle purlwise with the yarn behind the stitch.

## PATTERN DIAGRAM
Measurements in cm (in)

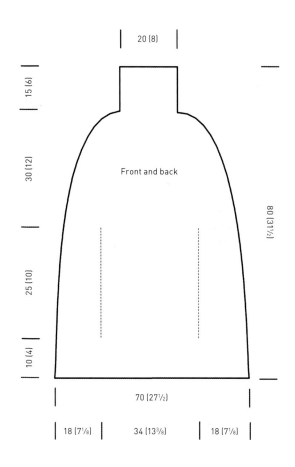

Front and back

20 (8)

15 (6)

30 (12)

25 (10)

10 (4)

80 (31½)

70 (27½)

18 (7⅛)   34 (13⅜)   18 (7⅛)

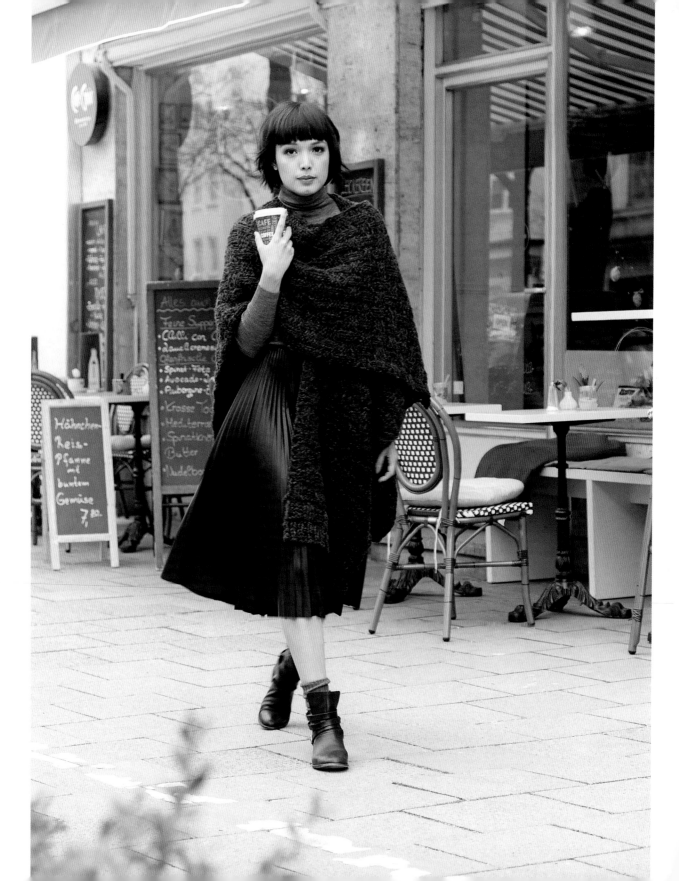

# All wrapped up

*CASUAL WRAP*

## TENSION
8 stitches and 12 rows in stocking stitch on 10mm (UK000/US15) needles = 10cm (4in) square.

## STITCHES
**Small basketweave pattern** | Work the small basketweave pattern from the chart on page 34 over multiples of 6 stitches + 2.
The figures to the right of the chart refer to the right-side rows, those to the left the wrong-side rows. Begin with the stitches before the first arrow, continue repeating the pattern (6 stitches) between the arrows and finish with the stitches after the second arrow. For clarity, three pattern repeats are shown. Work from the bottom of the chart up and keep repeating rows 1–12.
**Rib border** | Knit 1 purl 1 alternately.

## TO MAKE
The wrap is knitted in a single piece, beginning at the back hem and ending at the front hem.

**Back** | On a 10mm circular needle, cast on 86 stitches and work 5cm (2in) in knit 1 purl 1 rib. Then work from the chart and keep repeating rows 1–12.

Start the round with 2 stitches for the start of the pattern, then work 14 repeats of the 6 stitches between the arrows.

**Neck opening** | When work measures approximately 75cm (30in), after an 8th row of the chart, cast off the centre 10 stitches.

**Fronts** | Finish the right and left fronts separately. Leave the stitches for the left front

**CASUAL WRAP**
**One size**
**Style:** generous

**MATERIALS**
- 500g of Classic Elite Toboggan (80m/100g; 70% merino/ 30% alpaca) in black
- 10mm (UK000/US15) circular needle, 100cm (40in) long
- Circular needle to hold the stitches for the front

on a stitch holder and start with the right front. Continue the chart pattern as started on the back and work over 6 repeats plus 2 stitches for the pattern at the start of the row. When work measures 145cm (58in), finish with

5cm (2in) in knit 1 purl 1 rib.
Work the left front in the same way.

**Finishing** | Darn in all the ends.

# Chart and pattern

*CASUAL WRAP*

**CHART**
Small basketweave pattern

Key:

☐ = Knit 1
⊟ = Purl 1

**PATTERN DIAGRAM**
Measurements in cm (in)

Left front    Right front

50 (20)    10 (4)    50 (20)

5 (2)

70 (28)

150 (60)

Back

70 (28)

5 (2)

110 (44)

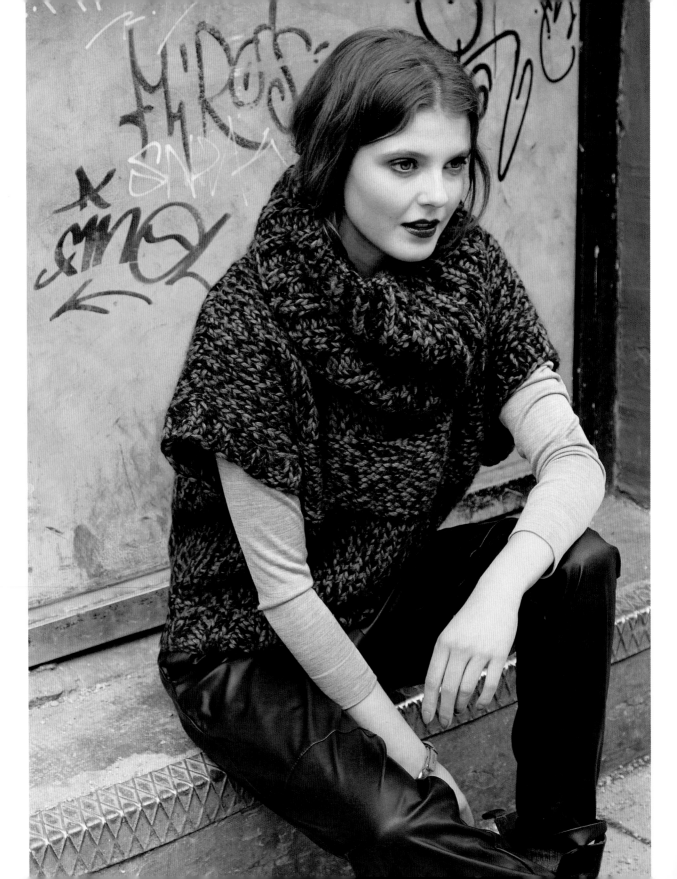

# Urban chic

*COSY TOP WITH MATCHING COWL*

## TENSION
9 stitches and 12 rows in stocking stitch
on 10mm (UK000/US15) needles = 10cm
(4in) square.

## STITCHES
**Stocking stitch** | In rows: Right-side rows knit
all stitches, wrong-side rows purl all stitches.
In rounds: Knit all stitches.
**Reverse stocking stitch** | In rows: Right-side
rows purl all stitches, wrong-side rows knit all
stitches.
In rounds: Purl all stitches.
**Rib borders** | Knit 2 purl 2 alternately.

## FOR THE TOP
The top is worked in rounds up to the armholes.

**Rib border** | With 10mm circular needle cast on
80 (88:96) stitches, join into a round and work
8cm (3¼in) in knit 2 purl 2 rib.

**Front and back** | Change to stocking stitch,
increasing 8 stitches evenly distributed in the
first round (88 (96:104) stitches).
Mark the imaginary side seams with stitch
markers or safety pins. The front and back each
have 44 (48:52) stitches. The rounds start at the
right front edge.

### COSY TOP WITH MATCHING COWL
Sizes S, M, L
Measurements for size S are in front
of brackets: sizes M and L are inside
brackets (M:L). If only one
measurement is given, it applies
to all sizes.
**Style:** generous
**Cowl:** 80cm (32in) circumference and
40cm (16in) wide

## MATERIALS
- 500 (600:700)g Lana Grossa
  Ragazza Lei Mouliné (40m/50g;
  100% wool) in anthracite marl
  (col. 662) for top and 200g for cowl
- 10mm (UK000/US15) circular
  needles, 60 and 80cm (24 and 32in)
  long
- Set of 10mm (UK000/US15)
  double-pointed needles
- Stitch markers or safety pins
- Stitch holder or spare needle
- Tapestry needle for sewing up

**Increasing at both sides** | The top has very wide shoulders; increases are worked at both sides. In every 4th round make 1 four times by working into the strands between the first and second stitches and the second-last and last stitches of the front and back, i.e. 4 stitches added in every increase round. Work these increases 9 (10:11) times. When all increases have been worked, there will be 62 (68:74) stitches each for the front and back, i.e. 124 (136:148) stitches in total on the needle.

**Pattern stripe on front** | When work measures 28 (30:32)cm (11 (11⅞:12½)in), on the front work 10cm (4in) in reverse stocking stitch for the front stripe, then change back to stocking stitch.

**Divide for back and front** | When work measures 32 (34:36)cm (12½ (13½:14¼)in) divide for the armholes and finish the back and front separately (62 (68:74) stitches each). Finish the back first, by working a further 20cm (8in) in stocking stitch in rows without shaping.

**Back shoulder slope** | As the shoulders are extra-wide, a small slope is worked. When work measures 52 (54:56)cm (20½ (21¼: 22)in), decrease at the start (outer edge) for two rows each in the following sequence: for size S decrease 2–2–3–3–5–6 stitches, for size M 2–2–4–4–6–6 stitches and for size L 2–3–4–5–6–7 stitches. Slip the remaining 20 stitches onto a spare needle for the back neck.

**Front neck** | When work measures 48 (50:52)cm (19 (19¾:20½)in), slip the centre 14 stitches onto a spare needle or a stitch holder.
Finish the right and left fronts separately. In every other row, cast off at the neck edge 2 stitches once and 1 stitch once.

Continue without further shaping until work measures 52 (54:56)cm (20½ (21¼:22)in), then work the shoulder decreases as described for the back.

**Join shoulder seams** | Join the shoulder seams with a tapestry needle, either by sewing with the wrong sides together or by grafting from the right side.

**Neck border** | With the set of double-pointed needles, pick up the 20 stitches of the back neck from the holder, 18 stitches down one side of the front neck opening, 20 stitches of the front neck (14 from the stitch holder plus the cast-off stitches on either side) and 18 stitches up the other side of the front neck opening (76 stitches). Work 3cm (1¼in) in knit 1 purl 1 rib in rounds, then cast off all stitches loosely.

The neck border is designed not to lie flat but to form a small stand-up collar. If you would prefer a flat border, pick up only 60 stitches instead of 76 when you work the neck border.

# Pattern

*COSY TOP*

**PATTERN DIAGRAM**
Measurements in cm (in)

68 (75:82)
(26¾ (29½:32¼))

23 (26.5:30)
(9 (10³⁄₈:11¾))

22 (8¾)

23 (26.5:30)
(9 (10³⁄₈:11¾))

14 (5½)

10 (4)

10 (4)

10 (4)

20 (8)

Front and back

28 (30:32)
(11 (11⁷⁄₈:12⁵⁄₈))

24 (26:28)
(9½ (10¼:11))

62 (64:66)
(24½ (25¼:26))

8 (3¼)

10
(11:12)
(4 (4³⁄₈:4¾))

48 (53:58)
(19¼ (20⁷⁄₈:22⁷⁄₈))

10
(11:12)
(4 (4³⁄₈:4¾))

**Sleeve border** | With the set of double-pointed needles, pick up 44 stitches around the armhole and work 3cm (1¼in) in knit 1 purl 1 rib in rounds, then cast off all stitches loosely.

**FOR THE COWL**

With 10mm circular needle, cast on 72 stitches and join into a round. Work 40cm (15¾in) in knit 2 purl 2 rib in rounds, then cast off all stitches loosely.

**Finishing** | Darn in all the ends.

# Streetwise cool

*LONG BLOCK-STRIPE CARDIGAN*

## TENSION
11 stitches and 16 rows in stocking stitch on 7mm (UK2/US10½) needles = 10cm (4in) square.

## STITCHES
**Stocking stitch** | In rows: Right-side rows knit all stitches, wrong-side rows purl all stitches. In rounds: Knit all stitches.
**Reverse stocking stitch** | In rows: Right-side rows purl all stitches, wrong-side rows knit all stitches.
In rounds: Purl all stitches.
**Rib borders** | Knit 1 purl 1 alternately.

## TO MAKE
**Pockets** | Start by knitting the pockets. They will be worked into the fronts of the cardigan later. Cast on 17 stitches in oatmeal and work 13cm (5¼in) in stocking stitch. When the pocket measures 13cm (5¼in), cast off the first two and last two stitches of the last right-side row. Slip the remaining 13 stitches onto a holder. Make the second pocket in the same way.

**Back and front** | The cardigan is knitted in one piece in rows as far as the armholes. With 7mm circular needle and dark grey marl, cast on 99 (111:123) stitches and work in knit 1 purl 1 rib. Start with a wrong-side row and purl 2 stitches, then knit 1 purl 1 alternately and end with purl 2.

## LONG BLOCK-STRIPE CARDIGAN
Measurements for size S are in front of brackets: sizes M and L are inside brackets (M:L). If only one measurement is given, it applies to all sizes.
**Style:** semi-fitted; narrow, but not constricting

## MATERIALS
- 100g Lana Grossa Yak Merino (110m/50g; 30% merino wool, 28% alpaca , 22% polyamide, 20% yak wool) in curry marl (col. 1), 250 (300:350)g in oatmeal (col. 10) and 300 (350:400)g in dark grey marl (col. 11)
- 7mm (UK2/US10½) circular needles 60 and 80cm (24 and 32in) long
- Set of 7mm (UK2/US10½) double-pointed needles
- Stitch markers or safety pins
- Stitch holders or spare needles
- 4 buttons, 25mm (1in) diameter

In the following rows work the stitches as they appear.

Work 8cm (3¼in) in rib.

Then change to curry marl and work 15cm (6in) in stocking stitch. Increase 1 stitch in the first stocking stitch row by knitting front and back into the 24th (27th:30th) stitch.

Divide the stitches as follows: 24 (27:30) stitches for the right front, 52 (58:64) stitches for the back and 24 (27:30) stitches for the left front. Mark the imaginary side seams with stitch markers or safety pins.

Note: The ribbed front border of the cardigan will be knitted on later and is 4cm (1½in) wide. (This is why the fronts added together have fewer stitches than the back.)

**Pockets** | When work measures 23cm (9in), change to dark grey marl and in the first dark grey row knit in the pockets as follows:

Knit 5 (6:7) stitches, slip the next 13 stitches onto a holder and knit the 13 stitches of the pocket from the holder, then knit the remaining 6 (8:10) stitches of the right front, the 52 (58:64) stitches of the back and 6 (8:10) stitches of the left front, slip the next 13 stitches onto a holder and knit the 13 stitches of the second pocket from their holder and finish the row by knitting the remaining 5 (6:7) stitches of the left front.

The pocket borders will later be knitted on the stitches from the holders.

Continue in stocking stitch, changing between oatmeal and dark grey every 8cm (3¼in).

**Decrease for the waist at both sides** | The cardigan is slightly waisted. Decreases for this are worked at both sides.

When work measures 45 (43:41)cm (17¾(17:16¼)in), knit together the third-last and second-last stitches of the right front (i.e. the 22nd and 23rd stitches for size S, the 25th and 26th stitches for size M and the 28th and 29th stitches for size L), the 2nd and 3rd stitches of the back, the third-last and second-last stitches of the back and the 2nd and 3rd stitches of the left front. 4 stitches are decreased in each decrease row.

Repeat the decreases twice more on every 8th row (88 (100:112)) stitches.

Work 7 rows and then start increasing again by knitting in the front and back of the 2nd stitch before and the 2nd stitch after the side seams. Repeat the increases twice more in every 8th row, until there are once again 100 (112:124) stitches on the needle.

**Front neck slope** | When work measures 63cm (24¾in), begin decreasing for the neck slope on both fronts and continue until only the 12 (14:16) stitches for the shoulders remain.

On the right front, decrease by working the third and fourth stitches as slip 1 knit 1 pass slipped stitch over, and on the left front by knitting together the fourth-last and third-last stitches.

For size S: Decrease on every 3rd right-side row.

For sizes M and L: Decrease in every 2nd and 3rd right-side row alternately.

Do not forget to start working the armholes when the work reaches 75 (73:71)cm (29½(28¾:28)in) in length.

**Divide for fronts and back** | When work measures 75 (73:71)cm (29½(28¾:28)in), begin casting off for the armholes and finish the back and fronts separately. Continue decreasing at the front neck edge as described on page 42. The centre 52 (58:64) stitches form the back, and the remaining stitches make up the right and left fronts. The number of stitches for the fronts may vary, depending on how many decreases have been worked.

**Back armhole** | Finish the back first. At the beginning of the next 6 rows, cast off 2 stitches four times and 1 stitch twice (42 (48:54) stitches remain). Continue working in stripe sequence.

**Back neck** | When work measures 94cm (37in), cast off the centre 18 (20:22) stitches. On each

side work 2 rows stocking stitch then slip the remaining 12 (14:16) stitches onto holders.

**Front armholes** | Work the armhole decreases as for the back, while continuing to decrease at the neck edge as before.
When work measures 95cm (37½in), slip the

# Pattern

*LONG BLOCK-STRIPE CARDIGAN*

## PATTERN DIAGRAM
Measurements in cm (in)

remaining 12 (14:16) stitches onto holders for the shoulders. They will later be knitted together with the shoulder stitches of the back.

**Join the shoulder seams** | Turn the cardigan to the wrong side and knit the shoulder stitches together by knitting 1 stitch of the back together with 1 stitch of the front each time. In the next row, cast off all stitches. Join the second shoulder in the same way.

**Pockets** | With dark grey yarn, pick up and knit the 13 stitches for the pocket border from the holder. Work 4cm (1⅝in) in rib. Then cast off all stitches. Sew the side edges invisibly to the fronts. On the wrong side, sew the pockets to the fronts with whip stitch, so that the seam does not show on the right side of the garment.

**Buttonhole and button band** | With dark grey marl yarn, pick up stitches evenly along the front edges and back neck. Work 2cm (¾in) in rib, beginning and ending at the hem edges with purl 1. On the next right-side row, 17cm (6¾in) from the hem of the right front, cast off 2 stitches for the first buttonhole. Make 3 more buttonholes in the same way, with 15cm (6in) between them. In the following wrong-side row, cast on 2 stitches over each buttonhole. When the band is 4cm (1⅝in) wide, cast off all stitches.

**Sleeves** | The sleeves are knitted in rounds on double-pointed needles, and have no seam. With dark grey marl and a set of 7mm double-pointed needles, cast on 24 (26:28) stitches and distribute the stitches evenly. Mark the imaginary seam.
Work 6cm (2⅜in) in knit 1 purl 1 rib.
Change to stocking stitch and work 12cm (4¾in) in curry marl.

Then continue in alternate 8cm (3¼in) stripes of oatmeal and dark grey.
Increase a total of 12 (14:16) stitches by knitting into the strand between the second and third stitches and between the third-last and second-last stitches of the round: for size S, in every 10th round 6 times; for size M, in every 8th round 7 times; for size L, in every 7th round 8 times; (36 (40:44) stitches on needles).

**Sleeve top** | When sleeve measures 50cm (19½in), change to working in rows, at first with two or three needles from the set. Later, one needle will be enough.
Cast off 2 stitches at the beginning of the next 4 rows and 1 stitch at the beginning of the following 2 rows (26 (30:34) stitches remain).
Cast off 1 stitch at each end of every 4th row 3 times (20 (24:28) stitches remain).
When sleeve top measures 11 (13:15)cm (4⅜ (5:6)in) from the start of the decreases, cast off at each side as follows:
For size S: for two rows each in the following sequence: cast off 1–1–2–3 stitches (14 stitches in total). Cast off the remaining 6 stitches in the next right-side row.
For size M: for two rows each in the following sequence: cast off 1–2–3–3 stitches (18 stitches in total). Cast off the remaining 6 stitches.
For size L: for two rows each in the following sequence: cast off 2–2–3–4 (22 stitches in total). Cast off the remaining 6 stitches.

**Finishing** | Sew in the sleeves. Darn in all the ends.

# Country style

ESCAPE TO THE COUNTRY WHERE THE FRESH BREEZE WILL BLOW
THOSE COBWEBS AWAY – AND IF THERE'S A NIP IN THE AIR, A
CHUNKY KNIT WILL KEEP YOU COMFY AND COSY

# Rustic charm

*HOODED JACKET WITH TOGGLES*

## TENSION
10 stitches and 15 rows in stocking stitch on 9mm (UK00/US13) needles = 10cm (4in) square.

## STITCHES
**Stocking stitch** | In rows: Right-side rows knit all stitches, wrong-side rows purl all stitches.
In rounds: Knit all stitches.
**Reverse stocking stitch** | In rows: Right-side rows purl all stitches, wrong-side rows knit all stitches.
In rounds: Purl all stitches.
**Rib borders** | Knit 1 purl 1 alternately.
**Cable pattern for sizes S and M** | Work from the chart on page 51. Work the 17 (19) stitch repeat between the arrows 5 times, ending with 18 stitches after the 2nd arrow (103 (113)) stitches. The figures to the right refer to the right-side rows; in the wrong-side rows, work the stitches as they appear. Work rows 1–63 once.
**Cable pattern for size L** | Work the 18 stitches between the arrows according to the chart on page 52. The figures to the right refer to the right-side rows; in the wrong-side rows, work the stitches as they appear. Work rows 1–63 once.

## HOODED JACKET WITH TOGGLES
**Sizes S, M, L**
Measurements for size S are in front of brackets: sizes M and L are inside brackets (M:L). If only one measurement is given, it applies to all sizes.
**Style:** semi-fitted; narrow, but not constricting

## MATERIALS
- 850 (950:1050)g Lana Grossa Mille II (55m/50g; 50% Wool, 50% acrylic) in Loden (col. 80)
- 9mm (UK00/US13) circular needles, 60 and 80cm (24 and 32in) long
- Set of 9mm (UK00/US13) double-pointed needles
- 6mm (UK4/US10/J) crochet hook
- Stitch markers or safety pins
- Stitch holder and cable needle
- 2 horn toggles

## TO MAKE

**Back and front** | The jacket is knitted in one piece in long rows up to the armholes.

**Rib border** | On a 9mm circular needle, cast on 93 (103:115) stitches and work 8cm (3¼in) in knit 1 purl 1 rib. Start with a wrong-side row, beginning and ending with 1 purl.
When work measures 8cm (3¼in), increase 24 (24:25) stitches evenly in a wrong-side row (117 (127:140) stitches).

**Positioning the cable pattern** | Allocate the stitches as follows:
7 stitches for the ribbed front border, 24 (27:30) stitches for the right front, 55 (59:66) stitches for the back, 24 (27:30) stitches for the left front, 7 stitches for the ribbed front border.
Number of repeats:
For size S: 6 repeats (5 repeats of 17 stitches and 1 of 18 stitches) = 103 stitches.
For size M: 6 repeats (5 repeats of 19 stitches and 1 of 18 stitches) = 113 stitches.
For size L: 7 repeats of 18 stitches = 126 stitches.
Mark the imaginary side seams with stitch markers or safety pins.
Work the cable pattern from the chart until the work measures 44cm (17⅜in) on row 59.

**Rib pattern for the waist** | In row 59, the cables are reduced from 6 stitches to 4, according to the chart (12 (12:14) stitches fewer).
At the same time, the 4 purl stitches before and after the cables are each reduced to 3 stitches, by working purl 2 together (12 (12:14) stitches fewer).
Work 16cm (6⅜in) on these 93 (103:112) stitches, working the stitches as they appear. Then work in stocking stitch, with only the first 7 and last 7 stitches in rib for the border.

**Equalise the stitch numbers** | To keep the garment symmetrical, increase 1 stitch in the right front and 0 (0:1) stitch in the left front in the first stocking stitch row (94 (104:114) stitches)

**Divide for fronts and back** | When work measures 70 (68:66)cm (27½ (26¾:26)in), divide for the armholes and finish the fronts and back separately. The centre 44 (48:52) stitches form the back, with 25 (28:31) stitches for each front (94 (104:114) stitches).

**Back armhole** | Finish the back first. At the start of the following 4 rows, work 2 rows of each of the following; cast off 2 stitches once and 1 stitch once (38 (42:46) stitches). Continue in stocking stitch without further shaping until the work measures 90cm (35½in).

**Back neck** | Slip the centre 18 stitches onto a holder for the hood and the 10 (12:14) stitches at each side onto separate holders for the shoulders. They will later be knitted together with the shoulder stitches of the fronts.

**Front armholes** | Finish the fronts separately (25 (28:31) stitches for each). Work the armholes as for the back (22 (25:28) stitches).

**Front neck** | On both fronts, when the work measures 75cm (29½in), slip the 7 stitches of the border onto a stitch holder and work the neck edge on the remaining 15 (18:21) stitches.
At the neck edge of the following right-side rows, slip 2 stitches 1 (2:2) times and 1 stitch 3 (2:3) times onto safety pins. Continue in stocking stitch on the remaining 10 (12:14) stitches.
When work measures 90cm (35½in), slip these stitches onto holders for the shoulders.

# Charts

*HOODED JACKET WITH TOGGLES*

**CHART**
Cable pattern for size S

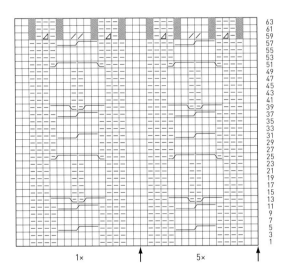

**CHART**
Cable pattern for size M

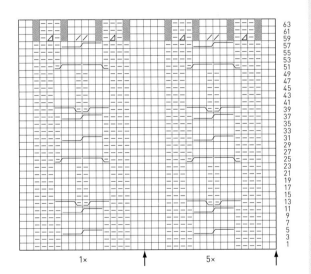

Key:

☐ = Knit 1
⊟ = Purl 1
⧄ = Knit 2 together
◪ = Purl 2 together
▨ = No stitch. Ignore when knitting

⊟▥▥▥ = Cross 4 right: Slip 1 stitch onto a cable needle and leave at back of work; knit 3, then purl the stitch from the cable needle

▥▥▥⊟ = Cross 4 left: Slip 3 stitches onto a cable needle and leave at front of work; purl 1, then knit the 3 stitches from the cable needle

▥▥▥▥▥▥ = Cross 6 right: Slip 3 stitches onto a cable needle and leave at back of work; knit 3, then knit the 3 stitches from the cable needle

# Chart

*HOODED JACKET WITH*
*TOGGLES*

**CHART**
Cable pattern for size L

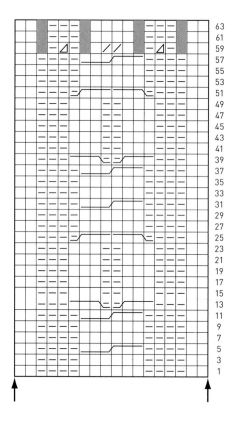

Key: see page 51

**Join the shoulder seams** | Turn the jacket to the wrong side and join one shoulder seam by knitting together 1 stitch of the back and 1 stitch of the front shoulder. Cast off the stitches one by one. Join the second shoulder seam in the same way.

Alternatively, the shoulder stitches can be grafted together or cast off and sewn up later.

**Hood** | For the hood, with the circular needle pick up the stitches as follows: pick up 7 stitches of the right border, 5 (6:7) stitches from the safety pins of the right neck edge, knit up 5 stitches along the side of the right neck, knit the 18 stitches of the back neck edge from the holder, knit up 5 stitches along the side of the left neck, slip 5 (6:7) stitches from the safety pins of the left neck edge, and 7 stitches of the left border (52 (54:56) stitches).

Continue in rows, working the border stitches in rib and the stitches in between in stocking stitch. In the second right-side row after picking up the stitches, decrease 2 stitches evenly distributed for size M and 4 stitches for size L by knitting 2 together (52 stitches on needle for all sizes). When hood measures 7cm (2¾in), after the 22nd stitch and before the 34th stitch, make 1 by knitting into the loop between stitches. Repeat these increases twice more in every 3rd row (58 stitches).

**Shortened rows at top of head** | Begin knitting shorter rows. Divide the stitches into 22 for the right side, 14 stitches centre strip and 22 for the left side. The 15 stitches to the right and left of the centre strip will gradually be decreased into the stitches of the border.

Rib the 7 stitches of the border, knit 15, knit 13 stitches of the centre strip, *slip 1, knit 1 (from the side panel), pass slipped stitch over. Turn. Slip the 1st stitch of the centre strip purlwise, purl 12, purl the last stitch of the centre strip together with the next stitch (from the side panel). Turn. Slip the 1st stitch knitwise, knit 12 *. Repeat from * to * until only the 7 stitches of the rib border remain on each side. Slip the centre 14 stitches onto a spare needle.

**Continue the borders** | Continue the right border on one needle, knitting the stitch at the end of the row together with the 1st stitch of the centre strip from the spare needle. Repeat 7 times in all. Continue the left border in the same way. When the borders meet in the middle, all the stitches of the centre strip will have been "used up". Cast off the borders and sew the ends together.

**Sleeves** | The sleeves are knitted in rounds on the set of 9mm double-pointed needles, and have no seam.
Cast on 20 (22:24) stitches and distribute evenly between the needles. Mark the imaginary seam. Work 8cm (3¼in) in knit 1 purl 1 rib.
Change to stocking stitch. Knit 1 round. In the next round, begin increasing by knitting into the strands between the second and third stitches and between the third-last and second-last stitches of the round, i.e. 2 stitches per round. Continue increasing in this way in every 6th round until there are 34 (36:40) stitches on the needles.

**Sleeve tops** | When sleeve measures 46cm (18⅛in), change to working in rows, to begin with on two or three needles from the set of double-pointed needles. Later, when fewer stitches remain, one needle will be enough.

At the start of the following 4 rows, work 2 rows each as follows; cast off 2 stitches once and 1 stitch once (28 (30:34) stitches remain). Continue decreasing 1 stitch at each end of every 4th row until 24 (26:30) stitches remain. When work measures 11 (13:14)cm (4⅜ (5¼:5½)in) from the start of the decreases for the top, at the beginning of the following 8 rows, work 2 rows of each of the following; cast off 1-2-2-4 stitches for size S; 1-2-3-4 stitches for size M; and 1-2-3-5 stitches for size L. On the next right-side row, cast off the remaining 6 (6:8) stitches.

**Fastening** | For the toggle loops, with double yarn and a 6mm crochet hook, make a chain 12cm (4¾in) long and fasten off the yarn. Form the chain into a U-shape. Sew 3cm (1¼in) together at the edges to make a loop 3cm (1¼in) long. The seam should be on the underside and will not be visible on the right side. Position the loop on the right front border, about 50cm (19¾in) from the hem, with the loop extending 2–3cm (¾–1¼in) beyond the border so that the toggle can easily be inserted through it, and sew on with single yarn. Make the second loop in the same way and sew on about 15cm (6in) higher up.
Sew the toggles to the left border, opposite the loops.

**Finishing** | Sew in the sleeves. Darn in all the ends.

# *Pattern*

*HOODED JACKET WITH TOGGLES*

**PATTERN DIAGRAM**
Measurements in cm (in)

# Spring break

*LONG TOP WITH COWL, WRISTWARMERS AND HAT*

## TENSION
11 stitches and 16 rows in stocking stitch on 7mm (UK2/US10½) needles = 10cm (4in) square.

## STITCHES
**Stocking stitch** | In rows: Right-side rows knit all stitches, wrong-side rows purl all stitches. In rounds: Knit all stitches.
**Reverse stocking stitch** | In rows: Right-side rows purl all stitches, wrong-side rows knit all stitches.
In rounds: Purl all stitches.
**Garter stitch borders** | In rows: Knit all stitches. In rounds: 1 round knit and 1 round purl alternately.

## FOR THE TOP
The top is knitted in rounds up to the armholes. With 7mm circular needle, cast on 112 (122:132) stitches, join into a round and work 4cm (1⅝in) in garter stitch.
Change to stocking stitch and reverse stocking stitch.

**Stitch allocation for front and back** | Front and back each consist of 5 bands of 11 (12:13) stitches, worked alternately in stocking stitch and reverse stocking stitch, starting and ending with knit stitches on the right side of work.

## LONG TOP WITH COWL, WRISTWARMERS AND HAT
Sizes S, M, L
Measurements for size S are in front of brackets: sizes M and L are inside brackets (M:L). If only one measurement is given, it applies to all sizes.
**Style:** generous
**Cowl:** 152cm (60in) circumference and 35cm (13¾in) wide
**Hat:** to fit head size 53–57cm (21–22½in)

## MATERIALS
- 300 (325:350)g Lana Grossa Yak Merino in fuchsia marl (col. 005) for top, 125g for cowl, 75g for hat and 25g for wristwarmers
- 7mm (UK2/US10½) circular needle, 80cm (32in) long
- Sets of 6mm (UK4/US10) and 9mm (UK00/US13) double-pointed needles
- Stitch holder or spare needle

Work 1 purl between the stitches of the front and back on each side to mark the side seams. Rounds begin at the right edge of the front. Stitch allocation: 55 (60:65) stitches for the front in bands, purl 1, 55 (60:65) stitches for the back in bands, purl 1.

**Kangaroo pocket** | When work measures 15cm (6in), on the front after the 15th (17th:20th) stitch of the round, make 1 by knitting into the strand between this stitch and the next stitch. Continue along the round, making 1 from the strand between each stitch 24 more times, then finish the round without further increases. In the next round, slip the 25 stitches just made onto a spare needle or stitch holder and leave at back of work and the original stiches onto a needle from a set of double-pointed needles at front of work. Working on these 25 stitches, finish the pocket first.
Work 26 rows, keeping the band pattern the same as before. On every 8th row, purl together the first two stitches and the last two stitches three times (19 stitches remain). After 26 rows, slip these stitches onto a holder.
Return to the top and work 26 rounds.
In round 27, knit 1 stitch of the pocket and 1 stitch of the top together – knit or purl, depending on the band pattern for each stitch of the pocket, and continue working in rounds on 112 (122:132) stitches.

**Increase for the wide sleeves** | When work measures 32cm (12⅝in), begin increasing for the sleeves, working the added stitches in the panel pattern, i.e. in reverse stocking stitch.
On front and back, on every 4th row/round, before and after the purl stitch marking the side seam, make 1 stitch by picking up and purling into the loop between the stitches, thus adding 4 stitches per round.
Repeat these increases 10 more times and then 0 (1:2) times on every 2nd row/round (156 (170:184) stitches on the needle).

**Divide for front and back** | When work measures 58cm (23in), change to working in rows and finish the back first.
Purl the stitches marking the side seams together with the neighbouring stitches, giving (77 (84:91) stitches) for the back and change to working in rows.
Slip the 77 (84:91) stitches for the front onto a spare needle.

**Back neck** | Continue without shaping until back measures 80cm (31½in). On the next row, cast off the centre 17 (18:19) stitches for the back neck. Slip the remaining 30 (33:36) stitches on each side onto holders for the shoulders. They will later be knitted together with the shoulder stitches of the fronts.

**Front neck** | Return to the front and work as for the back until the front measures 72cm (28¼in). Cast off the centre 9 (10:11) stitches for the neck. Finish the right and left sides separately, casting off at the neck edge on every other row 2 stitches once and 1 stitch twice.
When work measures 80cm (31½in), slip the remaining 30 (33:36) stitches onto holders. Knit the stitches of the front and back shoulders together on the wrong side. In the next row, cast off all stitches.

**Neck border** | With the set of 7mm double-pointed needles, pick up 60 stitches around the neck edge and work 4cm (1⅝in) garter stitch in rounds. Cast off all stitches loosely.

# Pattern

*LONG TOP*

**PATTERN DIAGRAM**
Measurements in cm (in)

70 (76:83)
(27½ (30:32¾))

27 (30:33)
(10¾ (12:13))

16 (16:17)
(6⅜ (6⅜:6¾))

27 (30:33)
(10¾ (12:13))

8
(3¼)

22 (8¾)

26 (10¼)

72 (28⅜)

80 (31½)

Front and back

32 (12⅝)

10
(11:12)
(4 (4⅜:4¾))

50 (54:59)
(19¾ (21¼:23¼))

10
(11:12)
(4 (4⅜:4¾))

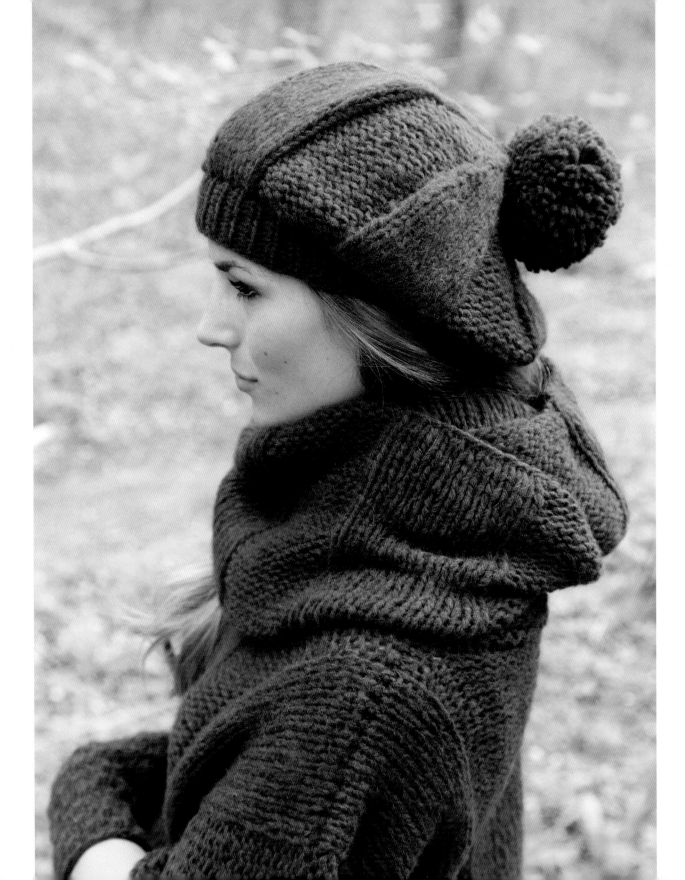

**Sleeve borders** | With the set of 7mm double-pointed needles, pick up 54 stitches around the armhole edge and work 4cm (1⅝in) garter stitch in rounds. Cast off all stitches loosely.

**Pocket borders** | With the set of 7mm double-pointed needles, pick up 20 stitches along the side edges and work 4cm (1⅝in) garter stitch in rows. Cast off all stitches loosely.
Sew the side edges to the front at the top and bottom of the pocket.

**Finishing** | Darn in all the ends.

### FOR THE COWL

The cowl is knitted in rounds.
With 7mm circular needle, cast on 168 stitches, join into a round, and work knit 12 purl 12 alternately.
When the work measures 35cm (14in), cast off all stitches loosely. Darn in all the ends.

### FOR THE WRISTWARMERS

On a set of 6mm double-pointed needles, cast on 26 stitches, distribute evenly and join into a round. Knit 1 round.
Then work in pattern:
Round 1: *Knit 2 together, yarn over needle; repeat from * to end of round.
Rounds 2–4: Work in stocking stitch.
Keep repeating rounds 1–4.
When work measures 24cm (9⅝in), cast off all stitches loosely and darn in all the ends.
Make a second wristwarmer in the same way.

### FOR THE HAT

The border is worked first, then the main part of the hat from the border up.

**Border** | On a set of 6mm double-pointed needles, cast on 60 stitches, distribute evenly, and join into a round.
Work in knit 1 purl 1 rib. Knit very tightly. After 4cm (1⅝in), cast off all stitches tightly.

**Top of hat** | With set of 6mm needles, pick up 90 stitches along the cast off edge of the band, picking up 1 stitch in the first stitch then 2 stitches in the next stitch, all the way around.
In round 1, work knit 9 purl 9 alternately, ending with purl 9.
Mark the beginning of the round.
Next round: Change to 9mm double-pointed needles. Work 12cm (4¾in) in the broad rib pattern, then start the decreases.

**Decrease for top of head** | 1st decrease round: Knit or purl together the first 2 stitches of all 10 "ribs" (80 stitches remain).
Work 1 round without decreasing.
2nd decrease round: Knit or purl together the last 2 stitches of all 10 ribs (70 stitches remain).
Work 1 round without decreasing.
Repeat the 1st and 2nd decreases together with the intervening non-increase round 3 more times, until 10 stitches remain on the needles.
Work a final round without decreasing, then cut the yarn, thread the end through all the stitches and draw together tightly. Darn in all the ends.

**Bobble** | Make a pom-pom (see page 137) about 8cm (3¼in) in diameter and sew it to the top of the hat.

# Shades of autumn

*LONG COAT WITH CABLE PATTERN*

## TENSION
10 stitches and 15 rows in stocking stitch on 10mm (UK000/US15) needles with yarn doubled = 10cm (4in) square.

## STITCHES
**Stocking stitch** | In rows: Right-side rows knit all stitches, wrong-side rows purl all stitches. In rounds: Knit all stitches.
**Staggered rib** | See also chart on page 65. In rows: Right-side rows knit 1, purl 1, wrong-side rows purl 1, knit 1. Work 4 rows, then change to right-side rows purl 1, knit 1 and wrong-side rows knit 1 purl 1. Continue in this way, changing every 4 rows.
**Diamond cable** | Work from the chart over the 14 stitches between the arrows. The figures to the right refer to the right-side rows. On wrong-side rows, work the stitches as they appear. Starting from the bottom, work rows 1–26 once, then keep repeating rows 5–26.
**Rib borders** | Knit 2 purl 2 alternately.

## LONG COAT WITH CABLE PATTERN
Sizes S, M, L
Measurements for size S are in front of brackets: sizes M and L are inside brackets (M:L). If only one measurement is given, it applies to all sizes.
**Style:** semi-fitted; narrow, but not constricting

## MATERIALS
- 800 (900:1000)g Lana Grossa Alta Moda Alpaca (140m/50g, 90% alpaca, 5% pure new wool, 5% polyamide) in grey-brown (col. 10)
- 10mm (UK000/US15) circular needles, 60 and 80cm (24 and 32in) long
- Set of 10mm (UK000/US15) double-pointed needles
- Stitch markers or safety pins
- Stitch holder or cable needle
- 1 button, 30mm (1¼in) diameter

## TO MAKE

The coat is knitted with double yarn.

**Back and front** | The coat is knitted in one piece in long rows up to the armholes. With 10mm circular needle and double yarn, cast on 85 (97:109) stitches.
Allocate the stitches as follows:
1 edge stitch, 19 (22:25) stitches for the front, 45 (51:57) stitches for the back, 19 (22:25) stitches for the left front, 1 edge stitch.
Mark the imaginary side seams with stitch markers or safety pins.
The pattern layout begins at the front edge of the right front: 1 edge stitch, 3 (4:5) stitches staggered rib, 14 stitches diamond cable pattern, 2 (4:6) stitches staggered rib, side seam marker, 5 (7:9) stitches staggered rib, 14 stitches diamond cable pattern, 7 (9:11) stitches staggered rib, 14 stitches diamond cable pattern, 5 (7:9) stitches staggered rib, side seam marker, 2 (4:6) stitches staggered rib, 14 stitches diamond cable pattern, 3 (4:5) stitches staggered rib, 1 edge stitch.

Note: The 8cm (3¼in) wide rib border is knitted on later. The fronts are therefore narrower than the back by half the width of the border, i.e. 4cm (1⅝in), so that the buttonhole and button will be at the centre front.

**Decrease for the waist** | The coat is slightly waisted. Decreases for this are worked at both side seams.
When work measures 50 (48:46)cm (19¾ (19:18⅛)in), knit together the third-last and second-last stitches of the right front, (i.e. for size S the 17th and 18th stitches, for size M the 20th and 21st stitches and for size L the 23rd and 24th stitches), the second and third stitches of

the back, the third-last and second-last stitches of the back and the second and third stitches of the left front.
4 stitches are thus decreased in each row.
Repeat the decreases twice more on every 6th row (73 (85:97) stitches remain). Work 7 rows and the increase again by knitting into the front and back of the 2nd stitch before and after the side seams. Repeat the increases twice more on every 8th row, (85 (97:109) stitches on the needle).

**Front neck** | When work measures 68cm (26¾in), begin decreasing at the neck edge on both fronts. On the right front, slip the third stitch, knit the fourth and pass the slipped stitch over, and on the left front, knit the third-last and fourth-last stitches together.
Decrease a total of 6 times on every 6th row. Remember to work the armholes as well, when the work measures 80 (78:76)cm (31½ (30⅝:30)in).

**Divide for fronts and back** | When work measures 80 (78:76)cm (31½ (30⅝:30)in), divide for the armholes and finish the fronts and back separately. Continue casting off at the front neck edges as described above.
The centre 45 (51:57) stitches form the back, the remaining stitches make up the right and left fronts. The number of stitches for the fronts may vary, depending on how many stitches have already been cast off at the neck edge.

**Back armholes** | Finish the back first. At the start of the following 6 rows, work 2 rows each as follows, cast off 2 stitches twice and 1 stitch once (35 (41:47) stitches remain). Continue in pattern.

# Charts and pattern

*LONG COAT WITH CABLE PATTERN*

## PATTERN DIAGRAM
Measurements
in cm (in)

## CHART
Diamond cable pattern

## CHART
Staggered rib pattern

Key:

☐ = Knit 1

⊟ = Purl 1

= Cross 3 right: Slip 1 stitch onto a
cable needle and leave at back of
work, knit 2, then purl the stitch
from the cable needle

= Cross 3 left: Slip 2 stitches onto a
cable needle and leave at front of
work, purl 1, then knit the 2 stitches
from the cable needle

**Back neck** | When work measures 98cm (38½in), cast off the centre 11 stitches. Cast off 3 stitches at each side of the neck on the next row. Slip the remaining 9 (12:15) stitches onto holders for the shoulders. They will later be knitted together with the shoulder stitches of the fronts.

**Front armholes** | Finish each front separately. Work the armholes as for the back. Continue decreasing at the neck edge. When work measures 100cm (39¾in), slip the remaining 9 (12:15) stitches onto holders for the shoulders. They will later be knitted together with the shoulder stitches of the back.

**Join the shoulder seams** | Turn the coat to the wrong side and join one shoulder seam by knitting together 1 stitch of the back and 1 stitch of the front shoulder. In the next (wrong-side) row, cast off all stitches. Join the second shoulder seam in the same way. Alternatively, the shoulder stitches can be grafted together or cast off and sewn up later.

**Front and neck border** | Pick up a total of 270 stitches along the front edges and the back of the neck, starting and ending with purl 2 at the hems. Work in knit 2, purl 2 rib. When 4cm (1⅝in) have been worked, make 1 buttonhole in the right front, 68cm (26¾in) up from the hem, by casting off 2 stitches. In the following wrong-side row, cast on 2 stitches to replace them and work a further 4cm (1⅝in). When the border is 8cm (3¼in) wide, cast off all stitches.

**Sleeves** | The sleeves are worked in rounds on double-pointed needles, and have no seams. On the set of 10mm double-pointed needles, cast on 20 (24:28) stitches and distribute evenly. Mark the imaginary seam.

Work 6cm (2⅜in) in knit 2 purl 2 rib. Change to working a diamond cable over the centre 14 stitches and the 3 (5:7) stitches on either side in staggered rib. Increase a total of 10 (12:14) stitches for the sleeves, by working 1 stitch into the strand between the second and third stitches and between the third-last and second-last stitches of the round (i.e. 2 stitches per round). Begin the increases in the 2nd round after the border. Increase a total of 5 (6:7) times in every 7th round working the increases in staggered rib (30 (36:42) stitches on the needles).

**Sleeve top** | When sleeve measures 50cm (19¾in), change to working in rows. To begin with, it is best to work on two or three needles from the set of double-pointed needles. Later, when fewer stitches remain, one needle will be enough. At the beginning of the following 6 rows, work 2 rows each of the following; cast off 2 stitches twice and 1 stitch once, (20 (26:32) stitches remain). Continue without shaping until sleeve measures 61 (63:64)cm (24 (24¼:25¼)in). Then at the start of the next 8 rows, work 2 rows each of the following; cast off 1–1–2–4 stitches for size S, 1–2–3–4 stitches for size M and 2–2–3–5 stitches for size L. Cast off the remaining 4 (6:8) stitches on the next right-side row.

**Finishing** | Sew in the sleeves. Darn in all the ends. Sew on the button.

# Winter warmers

*PONCHO WITH HAT AND LEGWARMERS*

## TENSION
10 stitches and 15 rows in stocking stitch on 10mm (UK000/US15) needles = 10cm (4in) square.

## STITCHES
**Stocking stitch** | In rounds: Knit all stitches.
**Rib borders** | Knit 2 purl 2 alternately.
**Diamond cable** | Work from the chart on page 71 over the 14 stitches between the arrows. The figures to the right refer to the pattern rows. On wrong-side rows, work the stitches as they appear. Starting from the bottom, keep repeating rows 1–28.
**Cable pattern** | Working from the chart on page 71, begin with the 6 stitches between the arrows. The figures to the right refer to the pattern rounds. On the rounds in between, work the stitches as stocking stitch. Starting from the bottom, work rounds 1 to 16 once, then repeat rounds 9–16 four times (48 rounds in total). Then work rounds 49–78 once.

## FOR THE PONCHO
The poncho is knitted in one piece in rounds from the bottom up, with a cable running down each arm.

**Rib border** | With the 100cm-long 10mm circular needle cast on 164 stitches and work 10cm (4in) in knit 2 purl 2 rib.

## PONCHO WITH HAT AND LEGWARMERS
**One size**
**Style:** generous
**Hat:** to fit head size 53–57cm (21–22½in)

## MATERIALS
- 500g Lana Grossa Alta Moda Super Baby in dark red (col. 20) for poncho, 100g for hat and 150g for legwarmers
- 10mm (UK000/US15) circular needles, 60, 80, and 100cm (24, 32, and 40in) long
- Sets of 9mm (UK00/US13) and 10mm (UK000/US15) double-pointed needles
- Safety pin or spare yarn
- 1 cable needle
- 1 fur bobble

69

**Stitch layout for the cables** | After the border, allocate the stitches as follows: 68 stitches stocking stitch for the back, 14 stitches for the left arm with diamond cable pattern from the chart, 68 stitches stocking stitch for the front, and 14 stitches for the right arm with diamond cable pattern from the chart. Mark the beginning of the rounds where the back meets the right arm. Work one round as described.

**Decreases** | Decrease by knitting together the second and third stitches and the third-last and second-last stitches of the stocking stitch back and front (i.e. 4 stitches in each decrease round). Work the decreases at the start of the back and front as slip 1, knit 1, pass slipped stitch over (see page 134) and those at the end as knit 2 together. Decrease in 2 successive rounds, then work 1 round without decreasing and repeat. This means that the number of stitches is reduced by 8 for every 3 rounds. Continue decreasing in this way until 52 stitches remain.

**Roll collar** | After an 18th round of the chart, when the work measures about 50cm (19¾in) and 52 stitches remain, change to knit 2 purl

2 rib for the roll collar. When the collar measures 24cm (9½in), cast off all stitches loosely.

**Finishing** | Darn in all the ends.

### FOR THE HAT

On the set of 9mm double-pointed needles, cast on 52 stitches and distribute evenly. Work 32cm (12⅝in) in knit 2 purl 2 rib (26 ribs).
Decrease for the top as follows:
1st decrease round: Purl together the two stitches of all the purl ribs (39 stitches remain). Work 1 round without decreasing.
2nd decrease round: Knit together the two stitches of all the knit ribs (26 stitches remain). Work 1 round without decreasing.
3rd decrease round: Knit 2 together, purl 2 together to end of round (13 stitches remain).
Knit 1 round.
Cut the yarn, leaving a long end, thread it through all the stitches, draw the top of the hat together and fasten off on the inside. Attach the fur bobble.

### FOR THE LEGWARMERS

The legwarmers are knitted from the knee down. On the set of 10mm double-pointed needles, cast on 40 stitches and allocate the stitches as follows: 6 stitches from the chart, *purl 2, knit 2*, repeat from * to * twice more, purl 2, 6 stitches from the chart, *purl 2, knit 2 *, repeat from * to * twice more, purl 2. Work rounds 1–16 of the chart with these repetitions 3 times in all. On round 53, reduce each of the cables to 4 stitches by knitting 2 stitches together twice, and continue working from the chart.
When work measures 34cm (13½in), cast off all stitches loosely. Darn in all the ends.
Make the second legwarmer in the same way.

**Tip**

The poncho can also be worn with the diamond cable pattern at the front and back, as shown in the photo on page 68.

# Charts and pattern

## CHART
Diamond cable pattern

27
25
23
21
19
17
15
13
11
9
7
5
3
1

Key:

☐ = Knit 1

☐ = Purl 1

☐ = Knit 2 together

☐ = Cross 3 right: Slip 1 stitch onto a cable
needle and leave at back of work, knit 2, then
purl the stitch from the cable needle

☐ = Cross 3 left: Slip 2 stitches onto a cable
needle and leave at front of work, purl 1, then
knit the 2 stitches from the cable needle

☐ = Cable 4 back: Slip 2 stitches onto a cable
needle and leave at back of work, knit 2, then
knit the 2 stitches from the cable needle

☐ = Cable 6 back: Slip 3 stitches onto a cable
needle and leave at back of work, knit 3, then
knit the 3 stitches from the cable needle

## CHART
Cable pattern for legwarmers

77
75
73
71
69
67
65
63
61
59
57
55
53

51
49
15
13
11
9
7
5
3
1

## PATTERN DIAGRAM
Measurements in cm (in)

25 (10)

24 (9½)

40 (15¾)

74 (29¼)

Front and back

10 (4)

80 (31½)

# Subtle neutrals

*JUMPER WITH HAT
AND CHILD'S SHOULDER WARMER*

## TENSION

8 stitches and 16 rows in garter stitch on 12mm (UKn/a/US17) needles = 10cm (4in) square.

## STITCHES

**Garter stitch** | In rows: Knit all stitches.
In rounds: 1 round knit and 1 round purl alternately.
**Rib border** | Knit 1 purl 1 alternately.
**Hat border** | Knit 2 purl 2 alternately.

## FOR THE JUMPER

**Back and front** | The jumper is worked in one piece in rounds up to the armholes. On the 10mm circular needle, cast on 80 (90:100) stitches, join into a round and work 5cm (2in) in knit 1 purl 1 rib. Mark the imaginary seams with stitch markers or safety pins. The front and back each consist of 40 (45:50) stitches. The rounds begin at the right edge of the front.
When ribbing measures 5cm (2in), change to the 12mm needle and garter stitch.

**Divide for front and back** | When work measures 45 (44:43)cm (17¾ (17⅜:17)in), divide for the armholes and finish the back and front separately, working in rows. Divide the front and back into 40 (45:50) stitches for each and finish the back first.

### JUMPER WITH HAT AND CHILD'S SHOULDER WARMER

**Sizes S, M, L**
Measurements are given as S (M:L)
If one measurement is given, it applies to all sizes.
**Style:** relaxed to oversized
**Hat:** to fit head size 53–57cm (21¼–22¾in)
**Shoulder warmer:** size 116–128cm (46⅜–51¼in)

### MATERIALS

• 800 (850:900)g Lana Grossa Ragazza Lei in cream (col. 14) for jumper, 120g for hat, and 180g for shoulder warmer
• 10mm (UK000/US15) and 12mm (UKn/a/US17) circular needles, 80cm (32in) long
• Sets of 9mm (UK00/US13), 10mm (UK000/US15) and 12mm (UKn/a/US17) double-pointed needles
• Stitch markers or safety pins
• Stitch holders or spare needles

# Pattern

**PATTERN DIAGRAM FOR JUMPER**
Measurements in cm (in)

45 (48:50)
(17¾ (19:19¾))

Sleeve

43 (17¼)

5 (2)

22 (25:25)
(8¾ (10:10))

2 (¾)

16 (18:19) (6⅜ (7¼:7½))

13 (16:20) (5¼ (6⅜:8))

16 (18:19) (6⅜ (7¼:7½))

2 (¾)

2 (¾)

10 (4)

20 (21:22) (8 (8⅜:8¾))

Front and back

53 (21¼)

60 (23¾)

45 (44:43) (17¾ (17⅜:17))

5 (2)

49 (56:62)
19¼ (22:24½)

**PATTERN DIAGRAM FOR SHOULDER WARMER**
Measurements in cm (in)

18 (7¼)

6 (2⅜)

23 (9¼)

Front and back

29 (11½)

50 (19¾)

**Armholes** | Back and front alike: Cast off 2 stitches at the beginning of the next two rows (36 (41:46) stitches remain). Continue without further shaping.

**Back neck** | When work measures 63cm (24¾in), cast off the centre 6 (9:12) stitches and finish each side separately by casting off 2 stitches at the neck edge on the following right-side rows. Slip the remaining 13 (14:15) stitches onto holders for the shoulders. They will later be knitted together with the shoulder stitches of the fronts.

**Front neck** | When work measures 53cm (21in), cast off the centre 6 (9:12) stitches. Finish the right and left sides separately by casting off 1 stitch twice at the neck edge on every other row. Continue without shaping until work measures 65cm (25½in) and slip the 13 (14:15) shoulder stitches onto holders as for the back.

**Join the shoulder seams** | Turn the jumper to the wrong side and join one shoulder seam by knitting together 1 stitch of the back and 1 stitch of the front shoulder. In the next (wrong-side) row, cast off all stitches.
Join the second shoulder seam in the same way. Alternatively, the shoulder stitches can be grafted together or cast off and sewn up later.

**Neck border** | On the set of 10mm double-pointed needles, pick up 6 (9:12) stitches of the back neck, 23 (20:17) stitches down the side of the front, 6 (9:12) stitches cast off for the front neck and 23 (20:17) stitches up the other side of the front. (58 stitches). Work 3cm (1¼in) in knit 1 purl 1 rib, then cast off all stitches loosely.

**Sleeves** | The sleeves are knitted in rounds, with no seam, on a set of double-pointed needles. With 10mm needles, cast on 18 (20:20) stitches, distribute evenly, and work 5cm (2in) in knit 1 purl 1 rib. Mark the imaginary seam. Change to the set of 12mm double-pointed needles and garter stitch. Increase in the 3rd round of garter stitch, and every following 7th round, by knitting into the strand between the second and third stitches and the third-last and second-last stitches of the round. Work a total of 9 (9:10) increases (36 (38:40) stitches). When work measures 48cm (19in), cast off all stitches loosely.

**Finishing** | Sew in the sleeves. Darn in all the ends.

## FOR THE HAT

The hat is knitted from the border up.

With a set of 9mm double-pointed needles, cast on 40 stitches and distribute evenly.

Work 6cm (2⅜in) in knit 2 purl 2 rib. In the last round of the border, increase 5 stitches, evenly spaced (45 stitches). Change to the set of 12mm double-pointed needles and work in garter stitch, beginning with 1 round purl. Work 13cm (5¼in) in garter stitch.

When work measures 19cm (7½in) (border plus 13cm (5¼in)), begin decreasing for the top, until the last remaining stitches can be drawn together.

Note that the decreases are always worked on a purl round.

1st decrease round: Purl every 4th and 5th stitch together, then knit 1 round without shaping (36 stitches remain).

2nd decrease round: Purl every 3rd and 4th stitch together, then knit 1 round without shaping (27 stitches remain).

3rd decrease round: Purl every 2nd and 3rd stitch together, then knit 1 round without shaping (18 stitches remain).

4th decrease round: Purl 2 together to end of round (9 stitches remain).

Cut the yarn, leaving an end about 50cm (20in) long and thread this through the remaining stitches. Draw tight, bring the yarn end through to the wrong side and darn in firmly.

Darn in all other ends.

## FOR THE SHOULDER WARMER

With the set of 12mm double-pointed needles, cast on 28 stitches, distribute evenly and work 6cm (2⅜in) in rounds in knit 1 purl 1 rib. In the last round of ribbing, increase 4 stitches evenly spaced (32 stitches).

Change to garter stitch.

Divide the stitches, marking the divisions with stitch markers: 10 stitches for the back, 6 stitches for the right sleeve, 10 stitches for the front and 6 stitches for the left sleeve.

The rounds begin at the join between the left sleeve and the back.

Increase in the front and back on every 3rd round 12 times, working make 1 stitch by knitting into the strand between the two stitches before the marker for the start of each sleeve, and after the marker for the end of each sleeve (i.e. 4 stitches on each increase round). The front and back will get wider, while the sleeves remain the same. When 23cm (9¼in) in garter stitch has been worked, there should be 80 stitches on the needles.

Cast off all stitches loosely and darn in the ends.

# Woodland walk

*CASUAL RIBBED JACKET*

## TENSION
11 stitches and 16 rows in knit 2 purl 2 rib on 8mm (UK0/US11) needles = 10cm (4in) square.

## STITCH
**Double rib** | In rounds: Knit 2 purl 2 alternately. In rows: Knit 2 purl 2 alternately. On wrong-side rows, work the stitches as they appear.

## TO MAKE
**Back and front** | The jacket is knitted in one piece in long rows up to the armholes. With the 8mm circular needle, cast on 154 (170:186) stitches and work in knit 2 purl 2 rib. Start with a wrong-side row, beginning and ending with purl 2.

**Stitch allocation for front and back** |
22 stitches for the right border, 27 (31:35) stitches for the right front, 56 (64:72) stitches for the back, 27 (31:35) stitches for the left front, 22 stitches for the left border.
Mark the imaginary side seams in the centre of a knit rib, so that the fronts and back begin and end with knit 1 on either side of the marker.
Work 56cm (22in) in rib without shaping.

## CASUAL RIBBED JACKET
Sizes S, M, L
Measurements for size S are in front of brackets: sizes M and L are inside brackets (M:L). If only one measurement is given, it applies to all sizes.
Style: casual and cosy

## MATERIALS
- 350 (400:450)g Lana Grossa Yak Merino (110m/50g; 28% alpaca, 30% pure new wool, 20% yak, 22% polyamide) in petrol (col. 3)
- 8mm (UK0/US11) circular needle, 80cm (32in) long
- Set of 8mm (UK0/US11) double-pointed needles
- Stitch holders or spare needles
- Stitch markers or safety pins

# Pattern

**PATTERN DIAGRAM**
Measurements in cm (in)

**Divide for back and fronts** | When work measures 56cm (22in), divide for the armholes, finishing the back and fronts separately.

**Back** | For the back, continue in rib on the centre 56 (64:72) stitches.
When work measures 76 (77:78)cm (30 (30⅜:30¾)in), cast off the centre 22 stitches, leaving 17 (21:25) stitches for each shoulder. Finish the shoulders separately as follows: At the armhole edge on every other row, slip first 5 (7:8) stitches, then 5 (7:8) stitches, and lastly 7 (7:9) stitches onto safety pins. They will later be knitted together with the shoulder stitches of the fronts.

**Fronts** | Finish the fronts separately. Continue in rib on 49 (53:57) stitches. When the work measures 76 (77:78)cm (30 (30⅜:31¾)in), slip the 17 (21:25) shoulder stitches at the armhole edge onto holders, as for the back. They will later be knitted together with the shoulder stitches of the fronts.

**Join the shoulder seams** | Turn the jacket to the wrong side and join one shoulder seam by knitting together 1 stitch of the back and 1 stitch of the front shoulder.
In the next (wrong-side) row, cast off all stitches. Join the second shoulder seam in the same way. Alternatively, the shoulder stitches can be grafted together or cast off and sewn up later.

**Finish the borders** | On both fronts, work 10cm (4in) in rib on the remaining 32 stitches without shaping. Cast off all stitches and sew the ends together. Sew the border to the back of the neck.

**Sleeves** | The sleeves are worked in rounds, with no seam, on the set of double-pointed needles. On the set of 8mm double-pointed needles, cast on 24 (26:28) stitches, distribute evenly and close into a round.
Note: The rib pattern will only divide exactly for sizes S and L at the start. Because of the increases, the rib pattern next to the "seam" will change several times.
Mark the imaginary seam with a stitch marker or safety pin.
Increase in every 7th round 9 times, by knitting into the strand between the second and third stitches and the third-last and second-last stitches of the round (42 (44:46) stitches). When sleeve measures 50cm (19¾in), cast off all stitches.

**Finishing** | Sew in the sleeves. Darn in all the ends.

# Nature lover

*MINI-WAISTCOAT IN MOSS STITCH*

**TENSION**
10 stitches and 15 rows in moss stitch on 10mm (UK000/US15) needles = 10cm (4in) square.

**STITCH**
**Moss stitch** | Knit 1 purl 1 alternately. On the next row, move along by 1 stitch, so purl the knit stitches and knit the purl stitches.

**TO MAKE**
**Back** | On a 10mm circular needle, cast on 43 (45:47) stitches and work in moss stitch.

**Increase for wide sleeves** | When work measures 18cm (7¼in), at the end of the next 6 rows, 2 rows each of the following: cast on 2–3–5 stitches, working the stitches into the moss stitch pattern (63 (65:67) stitches). Continue in moss stitch until work measures 39cm (15⅜in).

**Back neck** | Next row: Work 24 (25:26) stitches, cast off 15 stitches and work 24 (25:26) stitches.

**Fronts** | Slip the 24 (25:26) stitches for the right front onto a holder and finish the left front first. Work 17cm (6¾in) from the back neck in moss stitch. Then in every other row, at the side-seam edge, cast off 5–3–2 stitches, corresponding to the sleeve increases for the back (14(15:16) stitches remain).

When work measures 39cm (15⅜in) from the back neck, cast off all remaining stitches loosely. Work the right front to match.

**Finishing** | Place the back and fronts right sides together, and sew up the side seams. Darn in all the ends.

**MINI-WAISTCOAT IN MOSS STITCH**
Sizes S, M, L
Measurements for size S are in front of brackets: sizes M and L are inside brackets (M:L). If only one measurement is given, it applies to all sizes.
**Style:** casual

**MATERIALS**
- 250 (300:300)g Lana Grossa Mille II (55m/50g; 50% wool, 50% acrylic) in dark petrol blue (col. 23)
- 10mm (UK000/US15) circular needle, 80cm (32in) long
- Stitch holder or spare needle

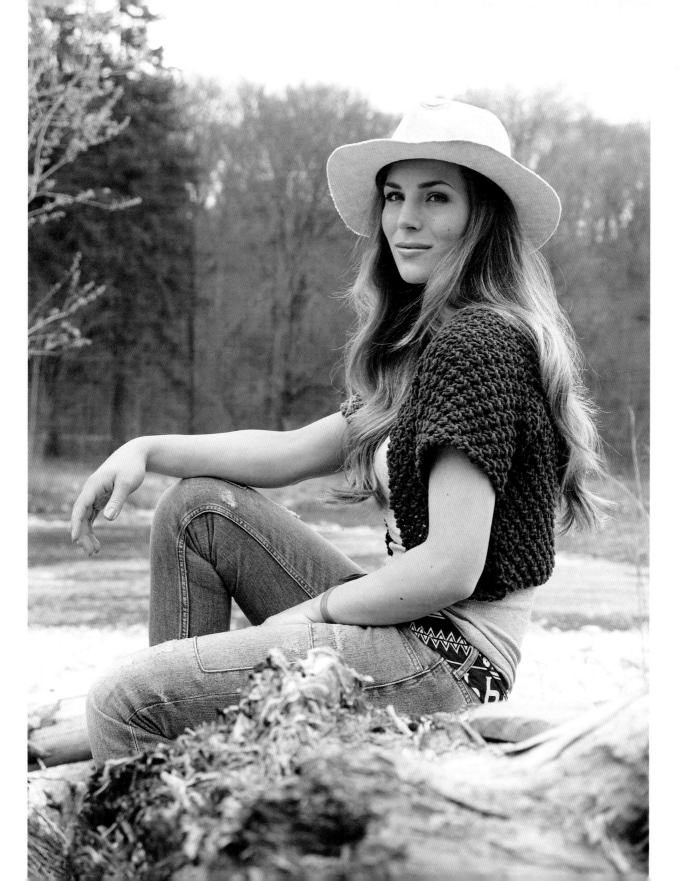

# Pattern

# Pattern

*MINI-WAISTCOAT*

*BODY WARMER*

## PATTERN DIAGRAM
Measurements in cm (in)

## PATTERN DIAGRAM
Measurements in cm (in)

63 (65:67)
(24¾ (25⅝:26⅜))

24 (25:26)
(9½ (10:10¼))

15 (6)

24 (25:26)
(9½ (9¾:10¼))

39 (15⅜)

Left front

Right front

78 (30¾)

17 (6¾)

4 (1⅝)

Back

18 (7¼)

10 (4)

43 (45:47)
(17 (17¾:18½))

10 (4)

Before folding

55 (21¾)

80 (31½)

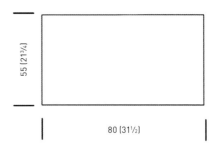

After folding

14 (5½) | 15 (6) | 22 (8¾) | 15 (6) | 14 (5½)

Seam

Seam

# Riverside ramble

*SIMPLE BODY WARMER*

**TENSION**
7 stitches and 9 rows in stocking stitch on
12mm (UKn/a/US17) needles with yarn tripled
= 10cm (4in) square.

**STITCHES**
**Stocking stitch** | Right-side rows knit all stitches,
wrong-side rows purl all stitches.
**Edge stitches** | Slip the 1st stitch of every row
knitwise and knit the last stitch.

**TO MAKE**
The yarn is used triple: Two strands camel/black
and one strand lilac/black.
With 12mm circular needle, cast on 56 stitches
and work in stocking stitch, beginning with a
wrong-side row (purl all stitches).
When work measures 55cm (21⅝in), cast off
all stitches loosely on a right-side row.

**Armholes** | Place the piece wrong-side up. Put
top right and bottom right edges together and
sew 15cm (6in) of the cast-on and cast-off edges
together. Do the same with the two left edges.
This produces a piece with armholes 14cm (5½in)
long and 28cm (11in) in circumference.

**Finishing** | Darn in all the ends.

**SIMPLE BODY WARMER**
One size
**Style:** casual
The size of the body warmer is easy
to change. The width of the piece
of knitting gives the width from
armhole to armhole. If you would
prefer the sleeves to reach to the
middle of the forearm, cast on about
20 more stitches. The height of the
piece of knitting gives the back
length.
For pattern diagram, see page 84.

**MATERIALS**
• 50g Lana Grossa Garzato Fleece
  (225m/50g; 70% alpaca, 30%
  polyamide) in lilac/black (col. 007)
  and 100g in camel/black (col. 006)
• 12mm (UKn/a/US17) circular
  needle, 80cm (32in) long

# Home comforts

IT'S THE WEEKEND AT LAST! ALL YOU NEED TO HELP YOU KICK
BACK AND RELAX IS A GOOD BOOK, A CUP OF FRAGRANT HERBAL
TEA... AND A COSY JUMPER TO SNUGGLE IN.

# Lazy days

*STOCKING-STITCH JUMPER WITH SCARF*

## TENSION

9 stitches and 15 rows in stocking stitch on 8mm (UK0/US11) needles = 10cm (4in) square.

## STITCHES

**Stocking stitch** | In rows: Right-side rows knit all stitches, wrong-side rows purl all stitches.
In rounds: Knit all stitches.
**Rib borders** | Knit 2 purl 2 alternately.

## FOR THE JUMPER

**Back and front** | The jumper is worked in one piece on the circular needle up to the armholes. On the 8mm circular needle, cast on 84 (92:100) stitches and work 8cm (3¼in) in knit 2 purl 2 rib. Change to stocking stitch.

**Divide for front and back** | When work measures 48 (47:46)cm (19¼(18¾: 18⅜)in), divide for the front and back, 42 (46:50) stitches for each. Continue in rows.

**Armholes** | Finish the back first. Cast off 4 stitches at the beginning of the next two rows (34 (38:42) stitches remain). Continue without shaping until work measures 66cm (26⅜in), then cast off all stitches.

### STOCKING-STITCH JUMPER WITH SCARF
Sizes S, M, L
Measurements for size S are in front of brackets: sizes M and L are inside brackets (M:L). If only one measurement is given, it applies to all sizes.
**Style:** semi-fitted
**Scarf:** 26cm (10¼in) wide, 200cm (80in) long

### MATERIALS

- 400 (450:500)g Lana Grossa Bombolo (65m/50g; 30% mohair, 20% pure new wool, 40% acrylic, 10% polyamide) in beige (col. 1) for jumper and 200g for scarf
- 8mm (UK0/US11) circular needle, 80cm (32in) long
- Set of 8mm (UK0/US11) double-pointed needles
- Stitch holders or spare needles

# Pattern

## STOCKING-STITCH JUMPER

**PATTERN DIAGRAM**
Measurements
in cm (in)

**Front neck** | Now finish the front. Cast off for the armholes as for the back (see page 91). When the work measures 50cm (19¾in), cast off the centre 10 stitches, leaving 12 (14:16) stitches on each side. Finish the right and left fronts separately. Cast off at the neck edge on every other row 2 stitches once and 1 stitch twice, or slip the stitches onto safety pins.
When work measures 66cm (26in), cast off 8 (10:12) stitches for the shoulders or slip them onto a holder.

**Sleeves** | Cast on 20 (24:24) stitches and either transfer to a set of double-pointed needles or knit the sleeve on two needles and sew up the seam later. Work 6cm (2⅜in) in knit 2 purl 2 rib, then change to stocking stitch.
In every 5th row, increase by making 1 in the

strand between the third and fourth stitches and the fourth-last and third-last stitches of the row. Work a total of 9 (8:9) increases (38 (40:42) stitches on needle). When sleeve measures 56cm (22in), cast off all stitches loosely.

**Finishing** | Sew up the shoulder and sleeve seams. Sew the sleeves in loosely. Pick up 40 stitches evenly around the neck edge and work 3cm (1¼in) in knit 2 purl 2 rib. Cast off all stitches loosely.

### FOR THE SCARF
With the 8mm circular needle, cast on 24 stitches and work in stocking stitch in rows. When the scarf measures 200cm (80in), cast off all stitches loosely.

# Sheer elegance

*PRETTY WRAPOVER CARDIGAN*

## TENSION
8 stitches and 13 rows in stocking stitch on 12mm (UKn/a/US17) needles = 10cm (4in) square.

## STITCHES
**Stocking stitch** | In rows: Right-side rows knit all stitches, wrong-side rows purl all stitches.
In rounds: Knit all stitches.

## TO MAKE
**Back and front** | The cardigan is worked in one piece in long rows up to the armholes. On the 12mm circular needle, cast on 102 (106:110) stitches and work 20cm (8in) in stocking stitch, starting with a purl (wrong-side) row.
Work the first stitch of every row as an edge stitch. On right-side rows, slip this stitch knitwise and on wrong-side rows, slip the first stitch purlwise.
The stitches are divided as follows: 15 stitches for the right front wrapover panel, 18 (19:20) stitches for the right front, 36 (38:40) stitches for the back, 18 (19:20) stitches for the left front, and 15 stitches for the left wrapover panel.
Mark the imaginary side seams with stitch markers or safety pins.

**PRETTY WRAPOVER CARDIGAN**
**Sizes S, M, L**
Measurements for size S are in front of brackets: sizes M and L are inside brackets (M:L). If only one measurement is given, it applies to all sizes.
**Style:** close-fitting

### MATERIALS
- 450 (500:550)g Lana Grossa Linea Pura Cashsilk (75m/50g; 15% silk, 15% cashmere, 30% viscose, 40% polyamide) in sage (col. 37 )
- 12mm (UKn/a/US17) circular needle, 80cm (32in) long
- Set of 112mm (UKn/a/US17) double-pointed needles
- 7mm (UK2/US10½) crochet hook or French knitter
- Stitch holders or spare needles
- Stitch markers or safety pins

# Pattern

**PATTERN DIAGRAM**
Measurements in cm (in)

**Hole for tie belt** | When work measures 20cm (8in), on a right-side row cast off the 33rd and 34th stitches and cast them on again in the following wrong-side row.

**Decrease for front edges** | Now, at the beginning of every right-side row, work the third and fourth stitches as slip 1, knit 1, pass slipped stitch over

and at the end of the row knit the fourth-last and third-last stitches together.

**Divide for fronts and back** | When work measures 42 (41:40)cm (16½(16¼: 15¾)in), divide for the armholes and finish the fronts and back separately. The centre 36 (38:40) stitches form the back. Divide the remaining

96

stitches by two for the fronts.
The number of stitches for the fronts will vary, depending on how many decreases have been worked.

**Back** | Finish the back first. Work without shaping until the back measures 60cm (23¾in), then cast off the centre 18 stitches and slip 9 (10:11) stitches at each side onto holders for the shoulders.

**Fronts** | Work as for the back, while continuing to decrease at the front edge until 9 (10:11) stitches remain on the needle. Slip these stitches onto holders.

**Join the shoulder seams** | Turn the cardigan to the wrong side and join one shoulder seam by knitting together 1 stitch of the back and 1 stitch of the front shoulder and cast off. Join the second shoulder seam in the same way.
Alternatively, the shoulder stitches can be grafted together or cast off and sewn up later.

**Tie belt** | With the 7mm crochet hook, make a chain 110 (115:120)cm (43¼ (45¼:47½)in) long and work a row of single crochet into it.
Alternatively, you could make a belt with a French

knitter or by twisting the yarn into a cord. Make a second belt in the same way and sew the belts to the fronts, 20cm (8in) from the bottom edge.

**Sleeves** | The sleeves are knitted in rounds with no seam, on the set of double-pointed needles. On the set of 12mm double-pointed needles, cast on 18 stitches, distribute evenly and mark the imaginary seam with a stitch marker or safety pin.

**Sleeve increases** | For size S, increase on every 4th round 6 times by making 1 in the strand between the second and third stitches and the third-last and second-last stitches (30 stitches on needles).
For size M, increase 7 times on every 4th round (32 stitches).
For size L, increase 8 times, in every 3rd and 4th round alternately (34 stitches).
When sleeve measures 60cm (23¾in), cast off all stitches.

**Finishing** | Sew in the sleeves. Darn in all the ends. Block according to instructions on ball band. Leave the cardigan to dry under a damp cloth.

# Soft and silky

*OPEN JACKET WITH MOSS-STITCH BORDERS
AND MATCHING SCARF*

## TENSION
9.5 stitches and 16 rows in stocking stitch on
10mm (UK000/US15) needles = 10cm (4in) square.

## STITCHES
**Stocking stitch** | In rows: Right-side rows knit all
stitches, wrong-side rows purl all stitches.
In rounds: Knit all stitches.
**Moss stitch** | Knit 1 purl 1 alternately. On the next
row, move along by 1 stitch, so purl the knit
stitches and knit the purl stitches.

## FOR THE JACKET
**Back and fronts** | The jacket is worked in one
piece in long rows up to the armholes. On 10mm
circular needle, cast on 104 (116:128) stitches and
work a 4cm (1⅝in) border in moss stitch.
Change to stocking stitch.
Divide the stitches as follows: 4 stitches for right
front border in moss stitch, 24 (27:30) stitches for
the right front, 48 (54:60) stitches for the back,
24 (27:30) stitches for the left front, and
4 stitches for the left front border in moss
stitch (104 (116:128) stitches).
Mark the imaginary side seams with stitch
markers or safety pins.

### OPEN JACKET AND MATCHING SCARF
Sizes S, M, L
Measurements for size S are in
front of brackets: sizes M and L are
inside brackets (M:L). If only one
measurement is given, it applies
to all sizes.
**Style:** casual, comfy
**Scarf:** 180cm (71in) long, 28cm
(11¼in) wide

### MATERIALS
- 500 (600:650)g Lana Grossa Linea
  Pura Cashsilk in lilac (col. 40) for
  jacket and 300g for scarf
- 10mm (UK000/US15) circular
  needles, 80 and 100cm
  (32 and 40in) long
- Set of 110mm (UK000/US15)
  double-pointed needles
- 12mm (UKn/a/US17) circular
  needle, 60cm (24in) long for scarf
- Stitch markers or safety pins
- Stitch holders or spare needles

**Front slope** | When work measures 38cm (15in), begin decreasing at both front neck edges. On the right front, work the second and third stitches after the border (i.e. the 6th and 7th stitches from the beginning of the row) as slip 1 knit 1, pass slipped stitch over (see page 134) and on the left front, knit together the third-last and second-last stitches before the border. Decrease on every 4th row a total of 9 times, until there are 15 (18:21) shoulder stitches plus 4 border stitches remaining on the needle. Remember to divide for the armholes when the work measures 50 (49:48)cm (20 (19⅝:19¼)in).

**Divide for fronts and back** | When the work measures 50 (49:48)cm (19¾ (19¼:19)in), divide for the armholes and finish the fronts and back separately. The centre 48 (54:60) stitches form the back.

**Finish the back** | Finish the back first, continuing to work in stocking stitch without shaping. When the work measures 70cm (27½in), cast off the centre 18 stitches and slip the remaining 15 (18:21) stitches at each side onto holders for the shoulders. They will later be knitted together with the shoulder stitches of the fronts.

**Finish the fronts** | Finish the fronts separately. Work in stocking stitch and continue decreasing as described above until 15 (18:21) shoulder stitches plus the 4 stitches of the border remain (19 (21:24) stitches). When work measures 70cm (28in), slip the 15 (18:21) knit stitches for the shoulders onto a holder. They will later be knitted together with the shoulder stitches of the back.

**Join the shoulder seams** | Turn the jacket to the wrong side and join one shoulder seam by knitting together 1 stitch of the back and 1 stitch of the front shoulder and casting off. Join the second shoulder seam in the same way. Alternatively, the shoulder stitches can be grafted together or cast off and sewn up later.

**Border** | Continue on the 4 stitches of the border for 10cm (4in) on each front, first increasing 1 stitch at the neck edge side, which will later be used as a seam allowance. Knit the ends of the borders together and sew the border to the back neck edge.

**Sleeves** | The sleeves are knitted in rounds with no seam, on double-pointed needles. On the set of 10mm double-pointed needles, cast on 24 (26:28) stitches and distribute evenly. Mark the imaginary seam with a stitch marker or a safety pin. Work 4cm (1⅝in) in moss stitch.

With this yarn, always start a new ball at the edge of a row, as the yarn structure means you cannot sew through the knitted stitches. Darned-in ends will be less visible at the edges of the work.

# Pattern

*OPEN JACKET WITH MOSS-STITCH BORDERS*

**PATTERN DIAGRAM**
Measurements in cm (in)

**Sleeve increases** | Work the increases by making 1 in the strand between the second and third stitches and between the third-last and second-last stitches of the round.
Increase at each end of every 7th round a total of 7 times (38 (40:42) stitches on needles).
When sleeve measures 50cm (19³⁄₄in), cast off all stitches loosely.

**Finishing** | Sew in the sleeves. Darn in all the ends.

On the 12mm circular needle, cast on 29 stitches.
Work in rows in moss stitch, beginning and ending each row with purl 1.
When the scarf measures 180cm (71in), cast off all stitches loosely and darn in the ends.

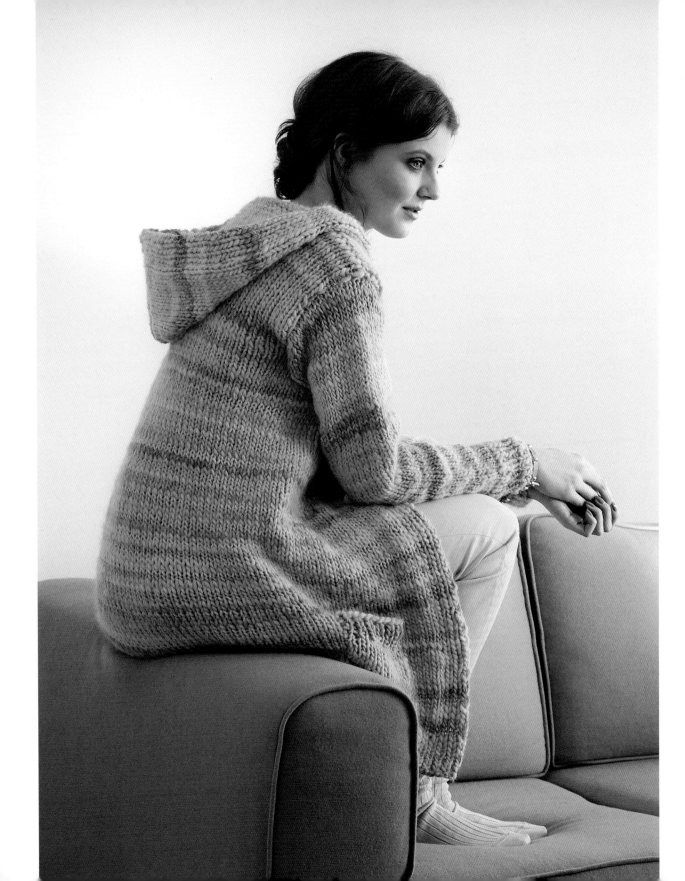

# Relax to the max

*LONG HOODED COAT*

## TENSION
9 stitches and 16 rows in stocking stitch on 9mm (UK00/US13) needles = 10cm (4in) square.

## STITCHES
**Stocking stitch** | In rows: Right-side rows knit all stitches, wrong-side rows purl all stitches. In rounds: Knit all stitches.
**Rib border** | Knit 1 purl 1 alternately.

## TO MAKE
**Back and front** | The coat is knitted in one piece in rows up to the armholes. On the 9mm circular needle, cast on 113 (125:137) stitches and work 6cm (2⅜in) in knit 1 purl 1 rib. Start with a wrong-side row, beginning and ending with purl. Change to stocking stitch, except for the rib borders. In the first row of stocking stitch, increase 1 stitch by knitting into the front and back of the 40th (43rd:46th) stitch.
The stitches are divided as follows:
6 stitches for the right front border in rib, 29 (32:35) stitches for the right front, 44 (50:56) stitches for the back, 29 (32:35) stitches for the left front, and 6 stitches for the left front border in rib (114 (126:138) stitches).
Mark the imaginary side seams with stitch markers or safety pins.

**LONG HOODED COAT**
**Sizes S, M, L**
Measurements for size S are in front of brackets: sizes M and L are inside brackets (M:L). If only one measurement is given, it applies to all sizes.
**Style:** casual, but not oversized

### MATERIALS
- 800 (900:1000)g Lana Grossa Olympia (100m/100g; 53% pure new wool, 47% Acrylic) in natural/beige (col. 413)
- 9mm (UK00/US13) circular needles 80cm (32in) long
- Set of 9mm (UK00/US13) double-pointed needles
- Stitch holders or spare needles
- Stitch markers or safety pins

# Pattern

*LONG HOODED COAT*

**PATTERN DIAGRAM**
Measurements in cm (in)

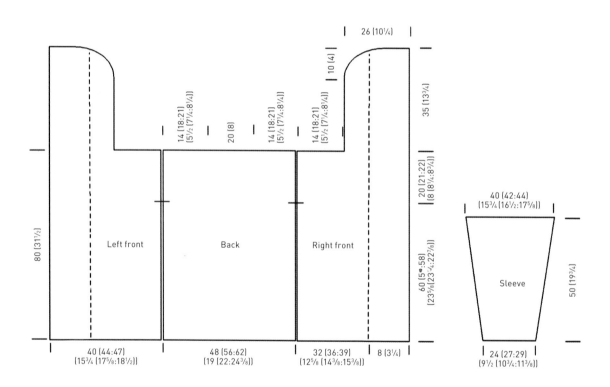

**Pockets** | On the 2nd right-side row after the border, slip the 12th–24th and 91st–103rd (103rd–115th:115th–127th) stitches onto stitch holders or spare needles. The pockets will be knitted later on these groups of 13 stitches. On the next wrong-side row, cast on 13 stitches above the gaps and continue working in stocking stitch.

**Divide for front and back** | When work measures 60 (59:58)cm (23⅝ (23¼:22⅞)in), divide for the armholes and finish the fronts and back separately.

**Finish the back** | Finish the back first, working in stocking stitch on the central 44 (50:56) stitches. When back measures 80cm (31½in), cast off the centre 18 stitches and slip the remaining 13 (16:19) stitches at each side onto holders for the shoulders. They will later be knitted together with the shoulder stitches of the fronts.

**Finish the fronts** | Finish each front separately. Work in stocking stitch over 29 (32:35) stitches, while continuing in rib on the first or last 6 stitches for the border. When the work measures 80cm (31½in), slip the 13 (16:19) stitches at the armhole edges onto holders for the shoulders.

**Join the shoulder seams** | Turn the coat to the wrong side and join one shoulder seam by knitting together 1 stitch of the back and 1 stitch of the front shoulder and cast off. Join the second shoulder seam in the same way. Alternatively, the shoulder stitches can be grafted together or cast off and sewn up later.

**Hood** | Pick up the remaining 22 stitches of the right front, 18 stitches from the back neck and 22 stitches of the left front on one needle (62 stitches). Continue working the border in ribbing and work the remaining stitches in stocking stitch.
Work 25cm (10in), then divide the stitches in two for the back and top of the head. Working outwards from the middle on both sides, in every second row cast off 2–3–4–5–6 stitches, so that a total of 20 stitches have been cast off on each half of the hood. Cast off the remaining 11 stitches. Sew the seam of the hood along the top of the head and down the centre back, in one continuous seam.

**Pockets** | Pick up the 13 stitches from the holders and work 12cm (4¾in) in stocking stitch and 3cm (1¼in) in rib. Cast off all stitches. Sew the pockets invisibly to the fronts.

**Sleeves** | The sleeves are knitted in rounds with no seam, on double-pointed needles.
On the set of 9mm double-pointed needles, cast on 22 (24:26) stitches and distribute evenly. Work 6cm (2⅜in) in rib.
Mark the imaginary seam.
Work the increases by making 1 in the strand between the second and third stitches and between the third-last and second-last stitches of the round.
Increase at each end of every 7th round a total of 7 times (36 (38:40) stitches on needles). When sleeve measures 50cm (19¾in), cast off all stitches loosely.

**Finishing** | Sew in the sleeves. Darn in all the ends.

# Snuggle up

*TWO-TONE JUMPER WITH BROAD STRIPES*

## TENSION

9 stitches and 15 rows in stocking stitch on
8mm (UK0/US11) needles = 10cm (4in) square.

## STITCHES

**Stocking stitch** | In rows: Right-side rows knit all
stitches, wrong-side rows purl all stitches.
In rounds: Knit all stitches.
**Rib border** | Knit 2 purl 2 alternately.
**Stripes** | Jumper: 5 stripes of 15cm (6in): old rose
for the ribbed border, then beige, old rose, beige,
old rose.
Sleeves: Old rose for the long cuff, one
15cm- (6in-) stripe in beige and the remainder
in old rose.

## TO MAKE

**Back and front** | The jumper is knitted in one
piece in rounds up to the armholes. On the 8mm
circular needle, cast on 96 (108:120) stitches in
old rose, join into a round and work 15cm (6in) in
knit 2 purl 2 rib.
Change to beige and stocking stitch. Keep an eye
on the stripe sequence.

### TWO-TONE JUMPER WITH BROAD STRIPES
**Sizes S, M, L**
Measurements for size S are in
front of brackets: sizes M and L are
inside brackets (M:L). If only one
measurement is given, it applies
to all sizes.
**Style:** oversized

### MATERIALS

- 200 (250:300)g Lana Grossa
  Bombolo 3U (65m/50g; 30%
  mohair, 20% pure new wool, 40%
  acrylic, 10% polyamide) in beige
  (col. 1) and 300 (350:400)g in old
  rose (col. 009)
- 8mm (UK0/US11) circular needle,
  80cm (32in) long
- Set of 8mm (UK0/US11) double-
  pointed needles
- Stitch markers or safety pins
- Spare needles or stitch holders

**Divide for front and back** | When the work measures 53 (52:51)cm (21 (20½:20)in), divide for the armholes and finish the front and back separately. Divide into 48 (54:60) stitches each for the front and back and change to working in rows. Finish the back first.

**Back** | Continue in stocking stitch until back measures 75cm (29½in), then leave the centre 20 stitches on a stitch holder or a spare needle. Cast off the 14 (17:20) shoulder stitches on each side loosely.

**Front** | Now finish the front. When front measures 63cm (24¾in), divide again for the neck and finish each side separately.

**Neck opening** | Slip the centre 12 stitches onto a holder. On every following alternate row, at the neck edge slip off 2 stitches once and 1 stitch twice onto safety pins (14 (17:20) stitches remaining on each side).
When work measures 75cm (29½in), cast off these shoulder stitches on each side.

**Shoulder seams** | Sew up the shoulder seams.

**Roll collar** | With a set of 8mm double-pointed needles and old rose, pick up the stitches from the front and back holders, knitting up 6 stitches from each of the neck edges in between (52 stitches). Work 35cm (13¾in) in knit 2 purl 2 rib, then cast off all stitches loosely.

**Sleeves** | On the set of double-pointed needles, cast on 24 stitches in old rose and work 24cm (9½in) in knit 2 purl 2 rib in rounds. Change to stocking stitch and beige. Mark the imaginary sleeve seam.

**Sleeve increases** | After the long cuff, work increases by making 1 in the strand between the second and third stitches and between the third-last and second-last stitches of the round. Increase at each end on every other round 8 (9:10)times in total (40 (42:44) stitches on needles). Remember to change back to old rose after completing a 15cm (6in) stripe in beige. When sleeve measures 54cm (21¼in), cast off all stitches.

**Finishing** | Sew in the sleeves. Darn in all the ends.

# Pattern

*TWO-TONE JUMPER WITH BROAD STRIPES*

**PATTERN DIAGRAM**
Measurements in cm (in)

# Light as air

*FLUFFY JUMPER WITH GIANT CABLE*

## TENSION
11 stitches and 15 rows in stocking stitch on
2mm (UKn/a/US17) needles with yarn doubled
= 10cm (4in) square.

## STITCHES
**Stocking stitch** | In rows: Right-side rows knit all
stitches, wrong-side rows purl all stitches.
In rounds: Knit all stitches.
**Rib border** | Knit 2 purl 2 alternately.
**Cable pattern** | Work from the chart over 30
stitches between the arrows. The figures to the
right refer to the right-side pattern rows or
rounds. When working in rounds, work all
non-cable stitches and rounds in knit: when
working in rows, work all wrong-side rows in
purl. Starting from the bottom, work rounds 1–54
once, then keep repeating rows or rounds 11–54.
Note: Only the odd-numbered rounds are shown
on the chart; work all the even-numbered rounds
or rows as described above, so that a cable is
knitted on every 22nd round.

## TO MAKE
Work with double yarn (one strand of each).

**Back and front** | The jumper is knitted in one
piece up to the armholes. On the 12mm circular
needle, cast on 120 (132:144) stitches and work

**FLUFFY JUMPER WITH GIANT
CABLE**
**Sizes S, M, L**
Measurements for size S are in
front of brackets: sizes M and L are
inside brackets (M:L). If only one
measurement is given, it applies
to all sizes.
**Style:** oversized

### MATERIALS
- 275 (300:325)g Lana Grossa Alta
  Moda Super Baby Fine (115m/25g;
  63% pure new wool, 27% alpaca,
  10% polyamide) in raw white/pale
  grey mix (col. 07)
  125 (150:175)g Lana Grossa
  Splendid (167m/25g; 72% mohair,
  21% nylon, 7% lurex) in raw
  white-silver (col. 12)
- 12mm (UKn/a/US17) circular
  needle, 80cm (32in) long
- Set of 12mm (UKn/a/US17)
  double-pointed needles
- Cable needle and stitch holders
- Stitch markers or safety pins

# Chart and pattern

*FLUFFY JUMPER WITH GIANT CABLE*

**PATTERN DIAGRAM**
Measurements in cm (in)

Front and back

16 (18:21)
(6³⁄₈ (7:8¹⁄₄)

24 (9¹⁄₂)

16 (18:21)
(6³⁄₈ (7:8¹⁄₄)

12
(4³⁄₄)

53 (21)

21 (22:23)
(8¹⁄₄ (8³⁄₄:9¹⁄₄)

65 (26)

44 (43:42)
(17¹⁄₄ (17:16⁵⁄₈)

56 (60:66)
(21⁵⁄₈ (23⁵⁄₈:26)

Sleeve

44 (46:47)
(17³⁄₈ (18:18¹⁄₂))

48 (19)

10 (4)

26 (10¹⁄₄)

**CHART**
Cable pattern

53
51
49
47
45
43
41
39
37
35
33
31
29
27
25
23
21
19
17
15
13
11
9
7
5
3
1

Key:
□ = Knit 1

= Cable 20 right: Slip 10 stitches onto a cable needle and leave at back of work, knit the next 10 stitches, then knit the 10 stitches from the cable needle.

= Cable 20 left: Slip 10 stitches onto a cable needle and leave at front of work, knit the next 10 stitches, then knit the 10 stitches from the cable needle.

10cm (4in) in knit 2 purl 2 rib.
Mark the imaginary side seams between front and back (60 (66:72) stitches for each). Change to stocking stitch and increase 14 stitches in the front by making 1 in the strand after every 4th stitch.
The front is 14 stitches wider than the back and now consists of 74 (80:86) stitches. The effect of the cable pattern will later make the two parts the same width.
Working the cable pattern over the centre

30 stitches, continue in stocking stitch until work measures 44 (43:42)cm (17¹⁄₄ (17:16⁵⁄₈)in).

**Divide for front and back** | When work measures 44 (43:42)cm (17¹⁄₄ (17:16⁵⁄₈)in), divide for the armholes, change to working in rows and finish the back and front separately.

**Back** | Finish the back first, continuing in stocking stitch on 60 (66:72) stitches. When work measures 65cm (25⁵⁄₈in), slip the centre 26 stitches onto a holder. Cast off the remaining 17 (20:23) stitches for each shoulder loosely or leave on stitch holders.

**Front neck** | Now finish the front. When front measures 53cm (21¼in), slip the centre 32 stitches onto a holder and finish the right and left neck edges separately.
In every following 2nd row, at the neck edge slip 2 stitches once and 1 stitch twice onto safety pins (17 (20:23) stitches remaining on each side). When work measures 65cm (25⅝in), cast off the shoulder stitches or leave on stitch holders.

**Shoulder seams** | Sew up the shoulder seams or knit them together.

**Roll collar** | On a set of double-pointed needles, pick up the stitches from the holders for the front and back neck, picking up 9 stitches in between along each side of the neck (76 stitches).
Work 15cm (6in) stocking stitch in rounds, continuing the cable pattern from the front. Cut the yarn, turn the jumper to the wrong side and attach the yarn again. Now on the wrong side, continue in stocking stitch with the cable pattern. This is so that when the collar is roughly turned down, the knit stitches and cable will appear on the right side.
When the collar measures 35cm (13¾in), cast off all stitches loosely.

**Sleeves** | The sleeves are long enough to allow the cuffs to be turned up. If you do not want to do this, make the sleeves about 8cm (3¼in) shorter.

**Sleeve border** | On the set of 12mm double-pointed needles, cast on 28 stitches and distribute evenly.
Work 10cm (4in) in rounds in knit 2 purl 2 rib.

Change to stocking stitch and increase 14 stitches evenly in the 1st round (42 stitches on needles). Mark the imaginary sleeve seam. The centre 30 stitches will be worked in the cable pattern.

**Sleeve increases** | Work the increases by making 1 in the strand between the second and third stitches and between the third-last and second-last stitches of the round, i.e. 2 stitches per round.
Increase at each end of every 6th round a total of 10 (11:12) times (62 (64:66) stitches on needles). When sleeve measures 56cm (22in), in the next round decrease over the 30 stitches of the cable area as follows: Knit 1, knit 2 together 14 times, knit 1. Continue in stocking stitch until sleeve measures 58cm (22¾in), then cast off all stitches loosely.

**Finishing** | Sew in the sleeves. Darn in all the ends.

Tip

To work out your own sleeve length, measure a suitably sized jumper from your wardrobe from one sleeve-edge up the sleeve, across the back and down to the bottom edge of the other sleeve. Then measure the back width of this jumper, subtract from the total and divide the remainder by 2.

# Easy earth tones

*LONG COAT WITH MULTI-COLOURED STRIPES
AND CHILD'S JUMPER*

## TENSION
10 stitches and 15 rows in stocking stitch on 10mm
(UK000/US15) needles with yarn doubled = 10cm
(4in) square.

## STITCHES
**Stocking stitch** | In rows: Right-side rows knit all
stitches, wrong-side rows purl all stitches.
In rounds: Knit all stitches.
**Rib border** | Knit 2 purl 2 alternately.
**Stripe sequence for back and front of coat** |
Work 8cm (3¼in) in rib in red-brown marl,
21 rows light green marl, 10 rows petrol marl,
14 rows blackberry/grey marl, 4 rows olive marl,
31 rows grey-brown, 4 rows light green marl,
11 rows petrol/royal marl, 10 rows red-brown
marl, 10 rows blackberry/grey marl, 4 rows
petrol marl, 15 rows light green marl, 9 rows
grey-brown.
**Stripe sequence for coat sleeves** | 8cm (3¼in) in
rib in red-brown marl, 4 rows olive marl, 31 rows
grey-brown, 4 rows light green marl, 11 rows
petrol/royal marl, 10 rows red-brown marl, 10
rows blackberry/grey marl, 4 rows petrol marl,
10 rows light green marl, 7 rows grey-brown.

## LONG KNITTED COAT
### Sizes S, M, L
Measurements for size S are in
front of brackets: sizes M and L are
inside brackets (M:L). If only one
measurement is given, it applies
to all sizes.

## MATERIALS
- Lana Grossa Alta Moda Alpaca:
  200 (250:300)g in taupe (col. 15),
  100g each in light green marl
  (col. 35) and grey-brown (col. 10);
  100 (150:150)g in red-brown marl
  (col. 29); 50g each in petrol/royal
  marl (col. 36), blackberry/grey
  marl (col. 20), olive marl (col. 43),
  and petrol marl (col. 08)
- 10mm (UK000/US15) circular
  needles, 60 and 80cm
  (24 and 32in) long
- Set of 10mm (UK000/US15)
  double-pointed needles
- Stitch markers or safety pins
- Stitch holders or spare needles
- 5 buttons, 20mm (¾in) diameter

## FOR THE COAT

The yarn is worked double, one strand of taupe plus one other colour as indicated.

**Pockets** | Work the pockets first. They will be knitted into the fronts of the coat later.
With the shorter 10mm needles and one strand each of light green marl and taupe, cast on 18 stitches and work 12cm (4¾in) in stocking stitch. On the last right-side row, cast off the first two and last two stitches. Slip the remaining 14 stitches onto a stitch holder. Make the second pocket in the same way.

**Back and front** | The coat is worked in one piece in long rows up to the armholes. With the 10mm circular needle and one strand of red-brown marl and one of taupe, cast on 88 (100:112) stitches. Begin with a wrong-side row and purl 3, then work in knit 2 purl 2 rib ending with knit 2, then purl the last 3 stitches.
Work 7cm (2¾in) in rib as set. Then change to light green marl and taupe and continue in stocking stitch. Keep to the stripe sequence. Allocate the stitches as follows: 21 (24:27) stitches for the right front, 46 (52:58) stitches for the back, and 21 (24:27) stitches for the left front. Mark the imaginary side seams with stitch markers or safety pins.

Note: The front border and shawl collar are knitted on later. The border is 4cm (1⅝in) wide. The fronts are 2cm (¾in) narrower than the back, i.e. half the width of the border, so that the buttonholes and buttons will be at the centre front. The number of stitches for the fronts is therefore less than half the number for the back.

**Attaching pockets** | When work measures 38cm (15¼in), on the first olive green row, knit in the pockets. Knit 5 (6:7) stitches, slip the next 14 stitches onto a stitch holder and knit across the 14 stitches of one pocket, knit the last 2 (4:6) stitches of the right front, the 46 (52:58) stitches of the back and 2 (4:6) stitches of the left front, slip the next 14 stitches onto a stitch holder and knit the 14 stitches of the second pocket, finishing the row with the remaining 5 (6:7) stitches of the left front. The pocket borders will later be knitted on the stitches from the holders. Continue in stocking stitch, keeping to the stripe sequence.

**Decrease for the waist** | The coat is slightly waisted. Decreases are worked at both sides. When work measures 56cm (22in), knit together the third-last and second-last stitches of the right front – i.e. the 19th and 20th stitches for size S, the 22nd and 23rd stitches for size M and the 25th and 26th stitches for size L – the second and third stitches of the back, the third-last and second-last stitches of the back and the second and third stitches of the left front. (4 stitches decreased per row).
Repeat these decreases twice more on every 6th row, (76 (88:100) stitches on the needle). Knit 7 rows, then increase in the next row by knitting into the front and back of the second stitch before and after both side seams.
Repeat these increases twice on every 8th row, (88 (100:112) stitches on the needle).

**Front neck slope** | When work measures 68cm (26¾in), start decreasing for the neck slope on both fronts. On the right front, slip the 3rd stitch, knit 1 and pass slipped stitch over; on the left front knit together the fourth-last and third-last stitches.
Decrease 7 times in all on every 6th row. Remember to divide for the armholes when work measures 80 (78:76)cm (31½ (30¾:30)in).

**Divide for fronts and back** | When the work measures 80 (78:76)cm (31½ (30¾:30)in), divide for the armholes and finish the fronts and back separately. Continue decreasing at the front neck edge as described above.

The centre 46 (52:58) stitches form the back, and the remaining stitches make up the right and left fronts. The number of stitches for the fronts may vary, depending on how many stitches have already been cast off at the neck edge.

**Back armhole** | Finish the back first. At the beginning of the following rows on each side, cast off 2 stitches twice and 1 stitch once (36 (42:48) stitches).

Continue in stripe sequence.

**Back neck** | When work measures 98cm (38½in), cast off the centre 12 stitches. On the next row on each side of the neck, cast off 3 stitches at the neck edge. Slip the remaining 9 (12:15) stitches for the shoulders onto holders. They will later be knitted together with the shoulder stitches of the fronts.

**Front armholes** | Finish the fronts separately. Work the armholes as for the back. Continue decreasing at the neck edge. When work measures 100cm (39¼in), slip the remaining 9 (12:15) stitches onto holders for the shoulders.

**Join the shoulder seams** | Turn the coat to the wrong side and join one shoulder seam by knitting together 1 stitch of the back and 1 stitch of the front shoulder and casting off one by one. Join the second shoulder seam in the same way. Alternatively, the shoulder stitches can be grafted together or cast off and sewn up later.

**Pocket borders** | For the pocket borders, work 4cm (1⅝in) in knit 2 purl 2 rib with one strand petrol marl and one strand taupe on the 14 stitches from the holder and cast off all stitches. Sew the side edges of the borders to the fronts. Sew the pockets to the inside of the coat fronts with whip stitch so the stitches cannot be seen on the right side.

**Shawl collar** | With blackberry/grey marl yarn, pick up 6 stitches up one side of the front neck edge, 4 stitches down from the shoulder seam at the side of the back neck, the 18 cast-off stitches of the back neck, 4 stitches up to the shoulder and another 6 stitches down the other side of the front neck (38 stitches).

Work a wrong-side row in knit 2 purl 2 rib. Turn and work the right-side row in rib. *At the end of the row pick up 2 more stitches on the front edge. Turn and pick up 2 more stitches at the end of the wrong side row *. Repeat from * to * until all the stitches have been picked up as far as the first front decrease (68cm (26¾in) up from the hem).

Now pick up stitches along the front edge on each side right down to the hem and work on all the stitches from hem to hem, beginning and ending every right-side row with knit 2 stitches at the hem edge.

**Front buttonhole border** | When border measures 2cm (¾in), on a right-side row, on the right front 3.5cm (1⅜in) from the hem, cast off 2 stitches for the first buttonhole. Make 4 more buttonholes 15cm (6in) apart, so that there are 5 buttonholes in all. On the following wrong-side row, cast on two stitches above the buttonholes. When the border measures 4cm (1⅝in), cast off all stitches.

# Pattern

**PATTERN DIAGRAM**
Measurements in cm (in)

**Sleeves** | The sleeves are knitted in rounds, with no seam. On the set of 10mm double-pointed needles, cast on 24 (24:28) stitches in red-brown marl and distribute evenly.

Mark the imaginary seam. Work 6cm (2³⁄₈in) in knit 2 purl 2 rib.

Change to stocking stitch and olive marl and keep to the stripe sequence.

For size M only: Increase 2 stitches, evenly spaced, in the first stocking stitch round.

Work sleeve increases by making 1 in the strand between the second and third stitches and between the third-last and second-last stitches of the round, i.e. 2 stitches per round.

Increase at each end of the second round of stocking stitch, then every 7th round, 4 (5:6) times in all, (32 (36:40) stitches on needles).

**Shape top** | When work measures 46cm (18in), change to working in rows, to begin with on two or three needles from the set of double-pointed needles. Later, when fewer stitches remain, one needle will be enough.

As for the front and back, at the beginning of the following rows on each side, cast off 2 stitches twice and 1 stitch once (22 (26:30) stitches remain).

Then cast off 1–1–0–1 stitches at the beginning of the next 8 rows (2 rows of each), (16 (20:24) stitches remain).

Continue without shaping until work measures 11 (13:15)cm (4³⁄₈ (5¹⁄₄:6)in) from the start of the armholes. At the beginning of each of the following rows, working 2 rows of each, cast off:

For size S: 1–2–3 stitches
For size M: 1–2–4 stitches
For size L: 1–3–5 stitches.

On the next row, cast off the remaining 4 (6:6) stitches.

**Finishing** | Sew in the sleeves. Darn in all the ends.

## FOR THE CHILD'S JUMPER

The yarn is worked double; one strand of taupe plus one other colour as indicated.

**Back and front** | The jumper is knitted in one piece in rounds up to the armholes.

On 10mm needles with one strand of petrol/royal marl and one strand of taupe, cast on 80 stitches and work 6cm (2³⁄₈in) in knit 2 purl 2 rib. Then change to stocking stitch with one strand of light green marl and one strand of taupe.

Keeping to the stripe sequence of 9cm (3⁵⁄₈in) in light green marl with taupe and 9cm (3⁵⁄₈in) in petrol/royal with taupe, continue in stocking stitch until work measures 36cm (14¹⁄₄in).

**CHILD'S JUMPER**
**Size 134–140 (9–10 years)**
**MATERIALS**
- Lana Grossa Alta Moda Alpaca (140m/50g; 90% alpaca, 5% wool, 5% polyamide): 200g in taupe (col. 15), 150g in light green marl (col. 35) and 150g in petrol/royal marl (col. 36)
- Set of 10mm (UK000/US15) double-pointed needles
- Stitch markers or safety pins
- Stitch holders or spare needles

# Pattern

*CHILD'S JUMPER*

**PATTERN DIAGRAM**
all measurements in cm

Front and back

2 (³/₄) | 9 (3⁵/₈) | 18 (7¹/₄) | 9 (3⁵/₈) | 2 (³/₄)

9 (3⁵/₈)

15 (6)

42 (16¹/₂)

45 (17³/₄)

36 (14¹/₄)

6 (2³/₈)

40 (15³/₄)

Sleeve

34 (13³/₈)

38 (15)

6 (2³/₈)

20 (8)

**Divide for front and back** | When work measures 36cm (14¹/₄in), divide for the armholes and finish the back and front separately. The back and front each consist of 40 stitches. Mark the imaginary side seams. Change to working in rows.

**Back armholes** | Finish the back first. Cast off 2 stitches at the start of the next 2 rows (36 stitches).
Continue in stripe sequence.

**Back neck and shoulders** | When work measures 51cm (20in), slip the centre 18 stitches onto a holder for the back neck and the outer 9 stitches at each side onto holders or spare needles for the shoulders.
The shoulder stitches will later be knitted together with the shoulder stitches of the fronts. The stitches of the back neck will be continued in the roll collar.

**Front armholes** | Work the armholes as for the back.
Continue straight until front measures 42cm (16½in).

**Front neck** | When front measures 42cm (16½in), slip the centre 12 stitches onto a stitch holder and finish the right and left fronts separately. At the neck edge of every other row, slip 2 stitches once and 1 stitch once onto safety pins for each side of the neck. Continue in stripe sequence on the remaining 9 stitches until front measures 51cm (20⅜in) and slip the stitches onto holders.

**Join the shoulder seams** | Turn the jumper to the wrong side and join one shoulder seam by knitting together 1 stitch of the back and 1 stitch of the front shoulder and casting off one by one. Join the second shoulder seam in the same way. Alternatively, the shoulder stitches can be grafted together or cast off and sewn up later.

**Roll collar** | On the set of 10mm double-pointed needles, with one strand petrol/royal marl and one strand taupe, pick up the 18 stitches of the back neck holder, 6 stitches down the front neck edge, the 18 stitches of the front neck from the holders and 6 stitches up the other side of the neck (48 stitches).
Work 10cm (4in) in knit 2 purl 2 rib on these 48 stitches, then cast off all stitches loosely.

**Sleeves** | The sleeves are knitted in rounds with no seam. On the set of 10mm double-pointed needles, with one strand petrol/royal marl and one strand taupe, cast on 20 stitches. Mark the imaginary seam.
Work 6cm (2⅜in) in knit 2 purl 2 rib.

Change to stocking stitch and one strand light green marl and one strand taupe and keep to the stripe sequence.
Change colour after every 9.5cm (3¾in) as for the front. In order to produce stripes of equal width, the stripes for the sleeve differ from those on the front by 0.5cm (³⁄₁₆in) per stripe.
Work the sleeve increases by making 1 in the strand between the second and third stitches and between the third-last and second-last stitches of the round, i.e. 2 stitches per round.
Increase at each end of the second round of stocking stitch, then every 6th round, a further 6 times (34 stitches on needles).
When sleeve measures 44cm (17⅜in), cast off all stitches loosely.

**Finishing** | Sew in the sleeves. Darn in all the ends.

# Luxurious lace

*PONCHO WITH MATCHING LEGWARMERS*

## TENSION
10 stitches and 15 rows in stocking stitch on 10mm (UK000/US15) needles = 10cm (4in) square.

## STITCHES
**Stocking stitch** | In rounds: Knit all stitches.
**Rib border** | Knit 2 purl 2 alternately.
**Large lace rib** | Work from the chart in rounds. Number of stitches divisible by 4. The figures to the right refer to the rounds. The precise allocation of stitches across the width is explained in the instructions. Keep repeating the pattern stitches between the arrows. Starting from the bottom, work rounds 1–24 once, then continue repeating these rounds, working the increased stitches on both sides into the pattern. Slipping the loop of the yarn over means the slipped stitch is extra-long, so it can comfortably stretch over 3 stitches.
**Hole pattern for the legwarmers** | Work from the chart. The precise allocation of stitches across the width is explained in the instructions. Keep repeating the pattern stitches between the arrows. For clarity, three pattern repeats are shown. Starting from the bottom, keep repeating rounds 1–24.

## PONCHO WITH MATCHING LEGWARMERS
**One size**
**Style:** generous

## MATERIALS
- 600g Lana Grossa Mille II (55m/50g; 50% wool, 50% acrylic) in antique violet (col. 066) for the poncho and 150g for the legwarmers
- 10mm (UK000/US15) circular needles, 60, 80, and 100cm (24, 32, and 40in) long
- 10mm (UK000/US15) double-pointed needles for the collar and legwarmers
- Stitch markers or safety pins

## FOR THE PONCHO

The poncho is worked in one piece in rounds from the top down, starting with the roll collar in knit 2 purl 2 rib and ending at the bottom hem with a rib border.

The rounds begin between the left arm and the back.

Mark the beginning of the rounds with a stitch marker or safety pin. Change to a longer needle when the number of stitches makes it necessary.

**Roll collar** | With the set of 10mm double-pointed needles, cast on 60 stitches and work 24cm (9½in) in knit 2 purl 2 rib.

**Stitch division for fast increases** | Divide the stitches into four areas of 15 stitches. Mark the four areas so you can see them more easily. Work 2 rounds of stocking stitch, then begin increasing. As shown in the chart, on every 4th round increase 2 stitches per "quarter", i.e. 8 stitches per round. The chart shows a quarter of a poncho. When 8 stitches have been increased in a quarter, a new pattern repeat will have been produced at each side.

Increase 8 times in every 4th round, so that after working 8 vertical pattern repeats, two new pattern repeats will have been produced at each side of each quarter (31 stitches per quarter, 124 stitches per round).

**Change to slower increases** | After working 8 vertical repeats, increase as shown in the chart 4 more times on every 8th round, by working yarn over needle after the first stitch and before the last stitch of each quarter.

This will produce 39 stitches per quarter (156 stitches per round).

Each quarter will now divide into knit 2, 9 repeats of 4 stitches, knit 1.

**Continue without shaping** | Continue on these 156 stitches as described above until the poncho measures 81cm (32in) (24cm (9½in) collar plus 57cm (22½in) in pattern).

**Bottom border** | When poncho measures 81cm (32in), work 5cm (2in) in knit 2 purl 2 rib, then cast off all stitches loosely.

**Finishing** | Darn in all the ends.

## FOR THE LEGWARMERS

The legwarmers are knitted in one piece in rounds from the bottom up, starting with a rib border at the ankle and ending with a rib border at the knee.

Mark the start of the rounds with a stitch marker or safety pin.

On a set of 10mm double-pointed needles, cast on 20 stitches and work 10cm (4in) in knit 2 purl 2 rib.

Next round: Change to stocking stitch and increase 8 stitches evenly over the round (28 stitches). Work 1 round stocking stitch.

Next and following rounds, work from the chart, repeating rounds 1–4 until the work measures 25cm (10in). The stitches between the arrows will be repeated 7 times per round. On the next 4 rounds, knit into the front and back of the last stitch (32 stitches).

There will now be 8 repeats per round instead of 7.

When work measures 40cm (15¾in), after a 4th round of the chart, work 1 more round in stocking stitch.

Finish the legwarmer with 8cm (3¼in) in knit 2 purl 2 rib and cast off all stitches loosely.

**Finishing** | Darn in all the ends.
Make a second legwarmer in the same way.

# Charts and pattern

## CHART
Large lace pattern for poncho

## CHART
Hole-pattern legwarmers

Key:

    ☐ = Knit 1 stitch

    Ⓞ = 1 yarn over

    ↓ = 1 new yarn over and drop the yarn over
        from the previous row.

    ▨ = No stitch. Ignore when knitting.

    ⊓⊓⊓⊓ = Work over 4 stitches: slip 1 knitwise, knit
        the next 3 stitches and pass the slipped
        stitch over the 3 knit stitches (= 3 stitches).

## PATTERN DIAGRAM FOR PONCHO
Measurements in cm (in)

# Basic techniques

WHETHER YOU'RE NEW TO KNITTING OR BRUSHING UP YOUR
SKILLS, THIS EASY-TO-FOLLOW GUIDE TO BASIC TECHNIQUES WILL
HELP YOU ACHIEVE GREAT RESULTS EVERY TIME.

## Casting on

**1** Make a slip knot around the needle, leaving a very long yarn tail. Hold the needle in your right hand, then loop the yarn tail over your left thumb and the ball yarn end round your left index finger. Hold both strands in place in the palm of your left hand.

**2** Insert the tip of the needle from under and up through the loop on your thumb.

**3** Wrap the tip of the needle round the loop on your forefinger from right to left, then use it to pull the yarn through the loop on your thumb.

**4** Slip your thumb out of the loop.

**5** Pull both yarn ends gently, to tighten the cast-on loop on the needle. Slide the new stitch up closer to the first slip-knot stitch.

**6** Loop the yarn around your thumb again and cast on another stitch by repeating Steps 2 to 6. Continue casting on until you have as many stitches as you need.

## Casting off knitwise

**1** Knit the first two stitches. Then insert the left needle into the first stitch and pull it up and over the second stitch, until it is off the right needle.

**2** Knit one more stitch, then repeat Step 1 to remove the stitch before it. Continue in the same way until only one stitch remains on the needle.

**3** Cut the yarn, leaving either a tail of 20 cm (8 in) to be darned in later, or a much longer tail to use for a future seam. Pass the yarn end through the remaining loop and pull it tight.

## Slipping stitches off the needle

**Using a stitch holder:** If you are setting stitches aside to work on later, slip them carefully onto a suitable-sized stitch holder. Your instructions should tell you whether to cut the yarn or keep it attached to the ball.

**Using a length of yarn:** If you don't have a stitch holder, you can use cotton yarn. Using a large tapestry needle, pull the yarn through the stitches as you slip them off the knitting needle. Knot the ends of the cotton yarn together.

## Slipping stitches

### Slipping stitches purlwise

**1** Always slip stitches purlwise unless you are instructed otherwise. Insert the right needle into the front of the loop on the left needle, as if to work a purl stitch.

**2** Slide the stitch onto the right needle without working it. The slipped stitch now sits on the right needle, with the right side of the loop at the front and the yarn at the back of the work.

### Slipping stitches knitwise

**1** Only slip stitches knitwise if you are working decreases or if instructed to do so. Insert the right needle from right to left through the front of the loop on the left needle.

**2** Slide the stitch off the left needle and onto the right needle without working it. The slipped stitch now sits on the right needle, with the left side of the loop at the front, unlike the worked stitches next to it.

## Reading charts

Some knitters prefer charts to written patterns as they are easy to read, and because the visual patterns of the stitch repeats can be easier to memorize. The number of stitches to cast on is usually indicated on the chart. If not, you can calculate the cast-on. Count the number of stitches in the repeat and cast on a multiple of that number, plus any end stitches outside the repeat.

Each square represents one stitch and each horizontal line represents a row. After casting on, work from the bottom of the chart up. Read odd-numbered rows (usually right-side rows) from right to left, and even numbered rows (usually wrong-side rows) from left to right. Work the edge stitches, then work the stitches inside the repeat as many times as instructed. Some symbols mean one thing in the right-side (RS) row and another in the wrong-side (WS) row.

When you have worked all the rows, start again at the bottom to begin the "row repeat" once more.

## Measuring tension

Before you start a project, knit a swatch so you can check you are knitting the correct stitch size (tension) for your pattern. If your finished work doesn't have the correct tension, the finished item may not fit.

**1** Using the recommended needle size, knit a swatch about 13 cm (5 in) square. Lay it flat and insert two pins 10 cm (4 in) apart. Count the number of stitches between the pins.

**2** Now count the number of rows to 10 cm (4 in) in the same way. If there are fewer rows and stitches than in the instructions, use smaller needles. If there are more, try larger needles. For your project, use the needle size that best matches the correct tension.

## Altering patterns

You can alter the length of garment patterns worked in plain garter or stocking stitch, but avoid altering armholes, necklines and the tops of sleeve heads. As sleeves and some bodies have shaping, these must be adjusted too. Here's how to lengthen a sleeve.

**1** Photocopy, draw, or trace the original pattern diagram. Write the new required length on your copy, for example 48 cm.
**2** Find the number of rows to 10 cm in the tension note. Divide that number by 10 to calculate the number of rows there are in 1 cm. For example, if there were 30 rows per 10 cm, there would be 3 rows per 1 cm.
**3** Multiply the required new length by the number of rows in 1 cm. The answer is the total number of rows in the new length – for example, 48 (cm) × 3 (rows per cm) = 144 rows.
**4** Any increasing will also have to be re-calculated. From the pattern, note the number of stitches to cast on at the cuff and how many there will be on the needle just before starting the underarm shaping. (This figure is often shown at the end of the instructions for the increases.)
**5** Subtract the smallest number from the largest number of stitches to be increased. Divide the answer by two (because a sleeve has two sides) to give the number of stitches to increase on each side. For example: 114 - 60 = 54 stitches. 54 ÷ 2 = 27. So 27 stitches would be increased at each side.
**6** To calculate the number of rows between each increase, divide the new number of rows found in Step 3 by the number of increases worked out in Step 5. If the answer is a fraction, round it down to a whole number. For example: 144 ÷ 27 = 4.22. So, you would increase one stitch each side every 4 rows. Knit the remaining rows straight before doing the underarm cast-offs.

## Increasing

### Knit into front and back of stitch

**1** Knit the stitch, but do not slip it off the left needle. Insert the right needle through the back of the loop from right to left.

**2** Wrap the yarn around the right needle, draw the yarn through to make a second stitch, then drop the old stitch off the left needle.

**3** In this way, two knit stitches are created from one and the row is increased by one stitch.

## "Make-one" left cross increase on a knit row

**1** With the left needle, pick up the horizontal strand between the stitch just knitted and the next stitch, as shown.

**2** Wrap the yarn around the tip of the right needle and draw the yarn through the lifted loop. This is called knitting through the back of the loop.

**3** There is now an extra stitch in the row. Knitting through the back of the loop creates a twist that closes up the hole that a new stitch would otherwise have created.

## Yarn over between knit stitches

**1** Bring the yarn forwards (yfwd) to the front between the needles. Take the yarn over the top of the right needle to the back, then knit the next stitch.

**2** When the knit stitch is complete, the yarn over is correctly formed on the right needle with the right leg of the loop at the front.

**3** In the next row, when you reach the yarn over, purl it through the front of the loop in the usual way. This creates a hole under the purl stitch.

## Decreasing

### Knit two together

**1** Insert the right needle knitwise from left to right through the second, and then the first stitch on the left needle.

**2** Wrap the yarn round the right needle, draw the yarn through both loops at the same time and slide both loops onto the right needle.

**3** This makes two stitches into one. The completed stitch slants to the right.

### Slip one, knit one, pass slipped stitch over

**1** Slip the first stitch from the left needle knitwise (see page 130). Knit the next stitch.

**2** Pick up the slipped stitch with the tip of the left needle. Pass it over the new knit stitch and off the right needle.

**3** The two stitches have become one stitch. The completed decrease slants to the left.

## Cables

Cables are usually knitted in stocking stitch on a reverse stocking stitch (or garter stitch) ground. They are made by crossing two, three or more stitches over other stitches in the row. Here the technique is illustrated with the cable 4 front and cable 4 back cables, which are crossed on every sixth row.

### Cable 4 front

**1** Work to the position of the four stocking stitches that form the cable. Slip the first two knit stitches that form the cable onto a cable needle. With the cable needle at the front, knit the next two stitches on the left needle.

**2** Next, knit the two stitches from the cable needle.

**3** This creates a cable crossing that slants to the left, which is why a front cable is sometimes called a left cable.

### Cable 4 back

**1** Work as for Step 1 of Cable 4 front, but hold the cable needle with the slipped stitches at the back of the work. Knit the next two stitches as normal.

**2** Then knit the two stitches from the cable needle.

**3** This creates a cable crossing that slants to the right. For this reason, a back cable is also known as a right cable.

## Horizontal inset pocket

**1** Make the pocket lining before you knit the garment piece. It must be two stitches wider than the cast off for the pocket. After working the last row, leave on the needle or slip onto a stitch holder.

**2** With the right side facing, work the main piece to the position of the pocket opening. Cast off knitwise the stitches for the pocket opening (see page 129), then knit to the end of the row.

**3** Turn and purl back to one stitch from the pocket position. Take the needle with the lining stitches in your left hand and purl the last main stitch and the first lining stitch together.

**4** Purl across the lining stitches. Purl the last stitch of the pocket together with the first one on the left needle. Finish working the main piece.

**5** As an alternative to Step 2, you could slip the opening stitches, without casting off, onto a stitch holder. Then you can knit an edging to the pocket later on.

**6** To make up the piece, sew the lining to the main piece with whip stitch, taking care not to pull the stitches too tight. This example has a contrasting colourway, but the lining would usually be made in the main yarn.

## Pom-poms

**1** On a piece of firm card, draw two circles 8 cm (3in) in diameter, then two circles of 2.5 cm (1 in) diameter in the centre of each. Cut out the circles so that you have two ring shapes. Now cut a few 1 m (1 yd) lengths of yarn and wind them together. Put the rings exactly on top of one another and start winding the yarn through the rings as shown.

**2** When the first ball of yarn runs out, make another and carry on winding. When the hole is completely filled, insert the tip of a pair of scissors between the pieces of card and start to cut the yarn around the outside of the ring.

**3** Continue cutting until all the wound strands of yarn have been cut along the outer rim of the ring. Now slide a long, doubled strand of yarn between the two pieces of card, then wrap and knot it tightly around the centre of the pom-pom.

**4** Carefully remove the pieces of card. Shake the pom-pom to fluff it up and trim into shape if necessary. Don't cut off the tie strands, as they can be used to sew on the pom-pom or hang it up. You can plump up your pom-pom even more by suspending it in steam for a short while (hang it off a knitting needle for safety.)

## Working on a set of five double-pointed needles

**1** Cast on the stitches on one needle, then distribute them evenly over four needles. Insert a marker between the first two stitches of the first round. Form the four needles into a square, taking care not to twist the cast-on row.

**2** Use the fifth needle to knit with. Work the first stitch of each needle tightly so that there are no gaps where you change from one needle to the next.

**3** When you have knitted all the stitches off the first needle, use the empty needle to work the stitches on the second needle. Continue working in this way, slipping the stitch marker from the left needle to the right when it is reached.

## Finishing

### Picking up stitches along a side edge

**1** For lightweight or medium-weight yarn, pick up about three stitches for every four row-ends. On the right side of the knitting, place a pin on the first of every four row-ends, as shown here.

**2** Insert the needle in the centre of the edge stitch and knit the stitches as you would when picking up along a cast-on edge. Skip every fourth row-end and remove pins before picking up stitches.

## Cast-off horizontal buttonhole

**1** On a knit row, work as far as the position of the buttonhole. Work two more stitches, then cast off knitwise however many stitches you need for the buttonhole (see page 129). When the last cast-off loop is on the right needle, slip the first stitch on the left needle onto the right needle and pass the cast-off loop over it. Knit to the end of the row. Turn, and work as far as the buttonhole.

**2** Drop the left needle (use a point protector to retain stitches if necessary). Hold the yarn and the right needle in your right hand. With your left thumb pointing down, pick up the yarn from behind, then wind your thumb to the right in an anticlockwise circle so the yarn crosses near the needle. Insert the right needle into the front thumb loop.

**3** Bring your left index finger from beneath, catching the yarn. Take the yarn left behind the needle, then wind it to the right, over the needle.

**4** Slip the thumb loop onto the right needle. Hold the loop with your right index finger and tighten the yarn with your left hand, making sure the loop goes all round the needle. Repeat for each cast-on stitch and knit to the end of the row.

**5** The horizontal buttonhole is finished.

## Joining seams

### Mattress stitch

**1** Ribbing and stocking stitch pieces can be sewn together almost invisibly with mattress stitch. Place the two pieces next to each other with the right sides facing up.

**2** Insert the needle from the front through the centre of the first knit stitch on one piece of work, then up through the centre of the stitch two rows above. Repeat on the other piece. Work from the bottom up, pulling the edges together.

### Grafting

Grafting can be used to join both cast-off edges and rows of stitches that have not been cast off.

**1** Place the pieces edge to edge with the right sides up. Work from right to left, inserting the needle through the stitches as shown.

**2** If you work in a matching yarn as shown here, the seam blends in completely. The result will look like a continuous piece of knitting.

## Blocking

When blocking (finishing a piece by steaming or pressing), always refer to your yarn label before you start. Textured patterns such as garter stitch, ribbing, and cables should be wet blocked or steamed very gently, so that you don't stretch or squash the pattern.

### Wet blocking

If the yarn allows it, wet blocking is the best way to even out your knitting. Wet or wash the piece in lukewarm water. Squeeze out gently, then roll up in a dry towel to squeeze out more moisture. Pin the piece into shape on a layer of dry towels covered with a sheet and leave to dry.

### Steam blocking

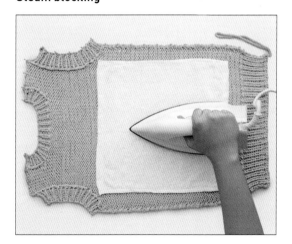

Only steam block if your yarn allows. Pin the piece into shape, then place a damp cloth on top. Use a warm iron to create steam, barely touching the damp cloth. Do not press the iron down on the knitting, and avoid any textured areas such as cables and ribbing. Leave the pins in place until the piece has dried completely.

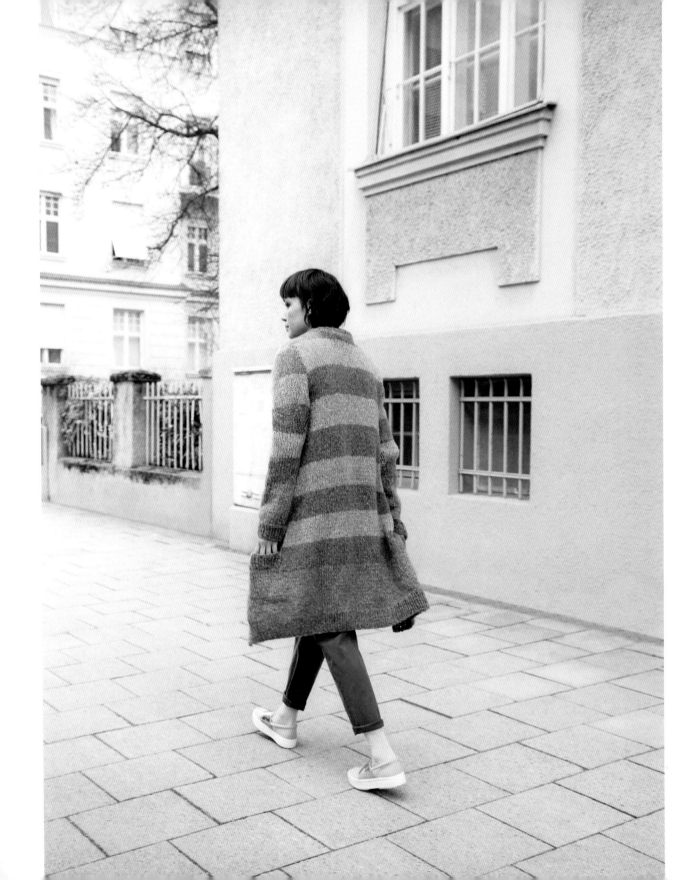

## About the author

Helgrid van Impelen has a degree in clothing technology; she is a fashion designer and a knitting and crochet junkie. Some years ago, after having abandoned craft activities for a long period during a busy phase in her career, she rediscovered knitting and crochet as the perfect way to relieve stress. Gradually, one book led to another and writing craft books now takes up the major part of her professional activities.

## Thanks

**Thanks from the author** | Grateful thanks to all the lovely busy knitters around me, especially to my mother, my aunt and my friend Anja. In addition, my thanks go to the firm of Lana Grossa and especially to Christine Lenz, who is always calm, often inspires me, and without whose unstinting help, many things would not be possible.

**Thanks from the publisher** | DK Verlag wishes to thank Lana Grossa (www.lanagrossa.de) for their support with the materials, Katja, Gina and Cora for their hard work during the photo shoots, Eva and Marcus for their photogenic flat and Irmi Eisenbarth of the Café "Das GaumenSpiel" (Franz-Joseph-Str. 30, 80801 Munich), where we were given permission to shoot some of the photos.

**Photography and styling** Katja Schubert, except for:
**Photos p. 8–9 and 128–141** DK Verlag
**Styling of models** Gina Pieper
**Hair and make-up** Corina Friedrich
**Models** Anne Wunderlich, Ana Saraiva Ludwig, Viktoria Fischer
**Charts** Edeltraut Söll
**Pattern diagrams** Helgrid van Impelen
**Illustrations** Derhajoe/Dreamstime (Schaf),
Dmstudio/Dreamstime (Wollknäuel), DeCe/Shutterstock (Schere)
**Editing** Anna Gülicher-Loll
**Layout, typography, realisation** Bettina Hoche

For DK Verlag
**Publisher** Monika Schlitzer
**Editorial management** Caren Hummel
**Project monitoring** Katharina May
**Production management** Dorothee Whittaker
**Production coordination** Arnika Marx
**Production** Inga Reinke

For DK UK
**Translation from German** Rae Walter in association with
First Edition Translations Ltd, Cambridge, UK
**Editor** Rona Skene
**Project Editor** Kathryn Meeker
**Senior Art Editor** Glenda Fisher
**Design Assistant** Philippa Nash
**Jacket Designer** Harriet Yeomans
**Senior Producer, Pre-Production** Tony Phipps
**Producer** Che Creasy
**Creative Technical Support** Sonia Charbonnier
**Managing Editor** Stephanie Farrow
**Managing Art Editor** Christine Keilty

First published in Great Britain in 2016 by
Dorling Kindersley Limited
80 Strand, London, WC2R 0RL

A CIP catalogue record for this book
is available from the British Library.
ISBN: 978-0-2412-5599-5

Printed and bound in China

All images © Dorling Kindersley Limited
For further information see: www.dkimages.com

A WORLD OF IDEAS:
SEE ALL THERE IS TO KNOW

**www.dk.com**